# TOWARDS THE GREAT COUNCIL

# TOWARDS THE GREAT COUNCIL

*Introductory reports of the Interorthodox Commission in preparation for the next Great and Holy Council of the Orthodox Church*

LONDON  SPCK

*English Translation*
*first published in 1972*
*by S.P.C.K.*
*Holy Trinity Church*
*Marylebone Road*
*London NW1 4DU*

*Second impression 1973*
*Printed in Great Britain by*
*The Talbot Press*
*Saffron Walden, Essex*

SBN 281 02739 0

# Contents

# Introduction

The documents published in this volume were drawn up by the Preparatory Commission of the Great and Holy Council of the Orthodox Church, during its first assembly held 16-28 July 1971 at the Orthodox Centre of the Ecumenical Patriarchate in Chambésy near Geneva.

The subjects which the Preparatory Commission was called upon to study theologically, were those proposed by the Fourth Panorthodox Conference held at Chambésy in 1968, taken from the list voted by the First Panorthodox Conference of Rhodes (1961). They are as follows:

1. From Chapter I 'Faith and Doctrine', under heading **B**:
   The Sources of Divine Revelation:
   (a) Holy Scripture:
      (i) Divine Inspiration of Holy Scripture.
      (ii) Authority in the Orthodox Church of the Old Testament Books known as Anaginoskomena.
      (iii) Critical edition of the Byzantine text of the New Testament.
   (b) Sacred Tradition (definition of its meaning and range).
2. From Chapter II 'Divine Worship', under heading **C**:
   Full participation by the laity in the worship and life of the Church.
3. From Chapter III 'Church Government and Order', under heading **E**:
   Adaptation of the ecclesiastical ordinances regarding fasting, to meet present-day needs.
4. From the same Chapter, under heading **G**:
   Impediments to marriage. A study of the present-day practice in the various local Churches and of the ecclesiastical procedure employed; also a means of securing, as far as possible, uniformity of practice on this matter throughout the whole of the Orthodox Church.

5. From the same Chapter, under heading I:
The Calendar question. A study relating the question to the decision of the First Ecumenical Council concerning Easter and seeking a way to re-establish a common practice among the Churches.
6. From Chapter VII 'Theological issues', under heading A:
Economy in the Orthodox Church.
   (a) Meaning of the terms 'Akribeia' and 'Oikonomia' in the Orthodox Church.
   (b) 'Oikonomia' (Economy):
       (i) In the sacraments within the Church and outside it.
       (ii) In the reception of heretics and schismatics by the Orthodox Church (some by baptism, some by anointing with Holy Chrism, some by a fresh confession of faith, some by a special form of prayer).
       (iii) In worship.

A theological study of each of the six subjects listed above was made as follows: the first, by the Church of Constantinople; the second, by the Church of Bulgaria; the third, by the Church of Serbia; the fourth, by the Church of Russia and the Church of Greece, separately; the fifth, by the Church of Russia and the Church of Greece, separately; and the sixth by the Church of Romania.

The reports made on these subjects were sent by the Churches concerned to the Secretariat for the Preparation of the Great and Holy Council of the Orthodox Church, which has its headquarters here at the Orthodox Patriarchal Centre. The Secretariat duly submitted these reports to all the local Churches, for their appraisal.

On the basis of the reports and their appraisal, the Interorthodox Preparatory Commission met to make a further study of the subjects and to reach an unanimous Orthodox viewpoint on each one of them.

In accordance with the procedure decided on by the Fourth Panorthodox Conference for preparing the Great and Holy Council, the introductory reports (or working reports) published in this volume are to be examined by a Preconciliar Panorthodox Conference, which will be summoned by the Ecumenical Patriarch with the agreement of the heads of the local Churches.

The Interorthodox Preparatory Commission has decided to ask the Ecumenical Patriarchate to convene the First Preconciliar Panorthodox Conference for the first fortnight of July 1972 at the Orthodox Patriarchal Centre here at Geneva.

The dossier on each of these six subjects, in the definitive form given it by this Conference, will be passed on by the Ecumenical Patriarch to the future Great and Holy Council, and stored in the archives of the Secretariat of the Preparatory Commission.

This First Preconciliar Panorthodox Conference will also select from the subject list of the Great Council thoses subjects which it intends to have studied during the second preparatory stage. In this way study of the subjects in stages will continue until all of them have been examined; then the Great and Holy Council will be convened.

Since the subject list has meantime undergone criticism, the Interorthodox Preparatory Commission 'has expressed a unanimous wish for the First Preconciliar Panorthodox Conference to review the subject list for the Great and Holy Council which the First Panorthodox Conference of Rhodes (1961) drew up'.

While the reports published here are the final introductory reports of the Interorthodox Preparatory Commission, they are not binding upon any conciliar decision. Through their publication and wide circulation, they are placed at the disposal of all the faithful members of the Church, who are called upon to develop a conciliar awareness and conscience, and to express their views, thereby participating actively in the work of preparing the Council.

The Secretariat of the Interorthodox Preparatory Commission has also been charged with the task of 'provoking reactions' on the work reports, and therefore welcomes all relevant contributions (Address: Secrétariat pour la preparation du Saint et Grand Concile de l'Eglise Orthodoxe, 37, chemin de Chambésy, 1292 Chambésy, Geneva, Switzerland).

Delivered at the Orthodox Centre of the Ecumenical Patriarchate on the 1st of November 1971.

✠ *Damaskinos, Metropolitan of Tranoupolis*
GENERAL SECRETARY

# 1

# *Divine Revelation and the way it expresses itself for the salvation of man*

After studying the subject chosen by the Fourth Panorthodox Conference in Chambésy, 'On the Sources of Revelation', the Interorthodox Preparatory Commission submits herewith to the First Preconciliar Panorthodox Conference for judgement and approval the present final draft of its preparatory report, as drawn up on the basis of the initial introductory report on the subject submitted by the Church of Constantinople, of the relevant views on the topic expressed beforehand by the Churches of Cyprus and Poland, and of the opinions voiced in assembly by the various delegates.

The final draft runs thus:

## I INTRODUCTION
## THE ONE AND ONLY REVELATION IN CHRIST

God, eternal and beyond comprehension, revealed in the Trinity and with us forever, 'is love' (1 John 4.8). And in His love, 'whose will it is that all men should find salvation and come to know the truth' (1 Tim. 2.4, NEB), it has pleased Him to encounter fallen man, and setting aside His own glory, to raise man up to divine bliss.

This being the eternal plan of the divine economy in the history of mankind, God has revealed Himself in many ways. In ancient times, He spoke 'in fragmentary and varied fashion' (Heb. 1.1), but 'when the term was completed', He spoke 'in the Son' (Gal. 4.4), revealing Himself personally to men, for their salvation.

This marvellous Revelation, one and unique, is directed towards man, embracing him completely. The divine revelation of God to man has taken many forms, unwritten in the oral tradition and written in Holy Scripture, but this diversity in no way points to a distinction of substance, but to a variety of forms. The Word of God, unveiled in the divine revelation and in His condescension coming down to us, is Himself the sole source of Revelation, just as He is the sole giver of salvation.

The one and only Word, being identical with the one source of Revelation, constitutes not only the foundation of faith for our Holy Orthodox Church, but also a dynamic force, since it is the incarnate Word of God who works all things in us (1 Cor. 12.6).

Revelation begins from the very moment God speaks to Adam and Eve, following their fall, and this is the first promise of God regarding future salvation (Gen. 3.15ff). It is continued and extended in the acts of divine intervention throughout the historical progress of Israel, from the making of the 'covenant' with Abraham (Gen. 17.2) down to the final bearers of God's spirit in the Old Testament. It reaches its climax, however, and its completion in Christ Jesus, who is the centre of God's saving work, and it is made perfect through the Incarnation, Passion and Resurrection of the Son, from which has proceeded the new filial communion of man with God, in Whose blood the new and eternal Covenant was established.

The 'gospel of Christ' (Gal. 1.7) was the full revelation of the religious truth granted by God to man. However great the part played by the Old Testament prophets and the Apostles in transmitting the revealed truth, yet it is in the same Jesus Christ that the essence of divine revelation is to be found, and its fulfilment. It is through this divine revelation that we Christians live even today, inasmuch as in these forms whereby divine revelation expresses itself, i.e. Holy Scripture (Old and New Testament) and Holy Tradition, the sum of our salvation is raised up, in Christ through His Church.

## II  HOLY SCRIPTURE

*The Old Testament*
Our Holy Orthodox Church honours not only the New but the Old Testament, since it also contains truths concerning faith and life revealed from on high and written under the guidance of the Holy Spirit, for the ordering and regulation of the works and thoughts of men according to the eternal counsels and ordinances of God, so that the law was 'a kind of tutor to conduct us to Christ' (Gal. 3.24). The Orthodox Church ascribes to the Old Testament the same validity and authority as that given it by our Lord and the Apostles, who themselves call the books of the Old Testament 'scriptures' (Matt. 21.42, 22.29, Luke 24.32, John 5.39, Acts 12.24) or 'the scripture' whenever dealing with particular passages of the Bible

(Luke 4.21, John 20.9, James 2.8), and also 'sacred scriptures' (Rom. 1.2) and 'sacred writings' (2 Tim. 3.15).

## 1. THE CANON OF THE OLD TESTAMENT

Our Holy Orthodox Church received the canon of the Old Testament from the Synagogue, but in addition to the canonical books contained in the Hebrew canon she makes use, both for public reading in church and for private study, of those books known as 'deuterocanonical' or 'Anaginoskomena' (literally 'The Books that are read').

The forming of this Old Testament canon, both in Israel and in a wider sphere, was a lengthy and toilsome process, varying according to time and place, and notably different among the Hebrews living in the promised land and among those at that time in the diaspora, when it came to judging what texts were or were not worthy of inclusion in the Old Testament canon. From this multifariousness there naturally arose contradictory opinions in the Church, both in ancient and more recent times, concerning the enumeration and the content of this canon. Our Holy Orthodox Church is aware that conflicting opinions have been expressed on this subject by her ecclesiastical writers and theologians. In order to terminate this conflict she now formulates what is the acceptable view, setting out the Old Testament as used by her, which comprises the 22 books of the Hebrew canon, subdivided into 39, and also the 10 Anaginoskomena, altogether 49 books. These are also distinguished into historical, doctrinal and prophetic, as follows: —

### A HISTORICAL:

(a) CANONICAL:

1. Genesis
2. Exodus
3. Leviticus
4. Numbers
5. Deuteronomy
6. Joshua
7. Judges
8. Ruth
9. I Kings
10. II Kings
11. III Kings
12. IV Kings
13. I Paraleipomena (Chronicles)
14. II Paraleipomena (Chronicles)
15. II Ezra (among the Slavs: I Ezra)
16. Nehemiah
17. Esther

(b) ANAGINOSKOMENA:

18. Judith
19. Hiereus or I Ezra (Slavs: II Ezra)
20. I Maccabees
21. II Maccabees
22. III Maccabees

### B DIDACTIC:

(a) CANONICAL:

23. Psalms
24. Job
25. Proverbs of Solomon
26. Ecclesiastes
27. Song of Songs

(b) ANAGINOSKOMENA:

28. Tobit
29. Wisdom of Sirach
30. Wisdom of Solomon

3

## C PROPHETIC:

### (i) Greater Prophets

(a) CANONICAL

31. Isaiah
32. Jeremiah
33. Ezekiel
34. Daniel
35. Lamentation of
    Jeremiah

(b) ANAGINOSKOMENA:

36. Epistle of Jeremiah
37. Baruch

### (ii) Lesser Prophets

38. Obadiah
39. Joel
40. Jonah
41. Amos
42. Hosea
43. Micah

44. Nahum
45. Zephaniah
46. Habakkuk
47. Haggai
48. Zachariah
49. Malachi

In the Slavonic edition, the book of III Esdras is numbered as the 50th Old Testament book, and is placed among the Anaginoskomena.

Our Holy Orthodox Church, according to the ancient order, does not accept those books known as apocryphal, considering them to be more recent and spurious, although some of them occur in certain codices of the Septuagint, notably in the Codex Alexandrinus.

## 2. THE AUTHORITY OF THE BOOKS KNOWN AS ANAGINOSKOMENA

With regard to the authority of those books known by her as Anaginoskomena, and used from the very beginning along with the canonical books of the Old Testament, the Eastern Orthodox Church declares and defines that these texts are to be distinguished from the canonical and inspired books as regards the authority of their divine inspiration, but that they are to be considered nevertheless as part of Holy Scripture, and useful and profitable to the faithful.

### The New Testament and its canon

Concerning the books held to constitute the canon of the New Testament, there are doubts, largely in the West and to a much lesser extent in our Orthodox East, which have not been resolved even today. Despite this, there are certain historical truths believed by the Church from the very beginning and forming in practice a conscious tradition of the Church. In virtue of these, the whole matter depends primarily on the common conscience of the faithful of our Church, and only in a secondary sense does it depend on scientific research and the clarification afforded by theological exegesis. In the past non-Orthodox scholars have often used negative criteria in their historical and critical research concerning the authenticity, purity, and canonicity of the New Testament books. But today historical and theological studies on the Bible, and the New Testament in particular, are adopting a more positive approach, which is proving undeniably productive in its results; and specialized historical and philological discussion of specific authors of the New Testament are tending to confirm the classical New Testament canon of 27 books, as established and maintained by tradition and accepted by our Holy Orthodox Church. It is this same Canon that she accepts and recognizes today as in the past.

## III THE DIVINE INSPIRATION OF HOLY SCRIPTURE

As regards the matter of inspiration, which is connected with the general question of the theology of Divine Revelation, our Holy Orthodox Church accepts the following teaching:

'Every scripture is inspired' (2 Tim. 3.16), says St Paul. This fact is witnessed to in many ways in the books of Scripture (see 1 Cor. 2.4, 13, Heb. 10.15, Apoc. 1.10-11, 14.12, 22.6), and it is also possible to find more general testimonies concerning the faith of the chosen people of God in the divine inspiration of the Scriptures, a faith at various times most lively among the people and its leaders, and especially so in our Lord and His Apostles (Exod. 24.4, Num. 33.2, Isa. 30.8, Jer. 36.2, 28, 32, II Mac. 2.13, 15 etc., Luke 4.17ff, Acts 1.16, Rom. 9.15 and 25, 1 Cor. 2.9–10, Heb. 1.5, 3.7, 10.16, Apoc. 14.13).

It is true to say that, at various times and in different authors, even in the pre-Christian period, the general theory of the divine inspiration of the sacred writers was taken up and dealt with, not only in connection with the New Testament but also with the Old. All the views expressed combine to demonstrate the truth of the Church's basic faith concerning the divine inspiration of the sacred writers. Our Holy Orthodox Church defines this as being the specific action of the Holy Spirit on the human consciousness and the human spirit; through it the whole man, in full possession of his faculties and expressing them actively in speech, writing, and composition, becomes a channel of communication for revelations from God according to the purposes of His eternal will.

In divine inspiration understood in this way, the active participation of the human faculties is presupposed, but special emphasis is to be placed upon the dominance of the divine element which is in all respects preponderant, the two blending harmoniously into one.

It is self-evident that, in this blending and collaboration; so far as the primary content of each revealed truth is concerned, the divine factor is predominant. And whenever there are unveiled to the human mind truths that are inaccessible and incomprehensible to it, divine inspiration and Revelation coincide. In this event, the participation of the human factor expresses itself only in the inscribing of the supernatural truths on the depths of the writer's consciousness; he then expresses them in a form appropriate to the human mind. When, however, the content of the revealed truths is such as to be knowable by other means as well, namely by natural revelation, then there is greater scope for human activity. Thus the divine inspiration of Holy Scripture is not excluded even when purely human thoughts and feelings occur in the sacred writers, inasmuch as the inspiration which is strictly divine, that is to say, the direct action of the Holy Spirit, concerns dogmatic and ethical truths alone.

As regards the outward form of Revelation, and notably the manner of its expression through phrases, words, arguments, the development of ideas, and general linguistic construction, the human element is acknowledged to play a greater part. It is specifically to this that we should attribute the personal 'seal' marked on the works of each sacred author. But at the same time Scripture in its entirety remains divinely inspired, seeing that the human spirit is moved in all these things by the action and guidance of the Holy Spirit that embraces it.

Therefore our Holy Orthodox Church declares that Scripture, being divinely inspired, preserves unimpaired within itself the presence of the Holy Spirit, in those revealed truths which it narrates, teaches and expounds for man's salvation. In its words it preserves intact the collaboration between the divine and the human factor in such a way that, even should the human presentation and clothing of God's word be imperfect, yet the substance of the divine content of the revelation is not impaired. The essence and distinctive character of both remain intact; the human element is to be investigated according to human methods, while the divine aspect is not to be formulated in a one-sided, individualistic, and subjective fashion, but all the details are to be judged in accordance with the entirety of Holy Scripture and Revelation, and this entirety in its turn is to be judged in accordance with the Tradition of the Church from the beginning, there being but one source for both the unwritten and the written divine word.

# IV   THE RESTORATION OF THE ORIGINAL TEXT
## OF THE NEW TESTAMENT BOOKS

As regards the discovery and restoration of the text of the New Testament books in its original form, and likewise as regards questions of authenticity, literary and historical worth, and the precise determination of the conditions of composition and other related problems, our Holy Orthodox Church recognizes that the surviving Greek manuscripts of the New Testament books—which amount to many thousands—present a variety of readings, yet without affecting the substance of the revealed truth; and the Church is able to distinguish and recognize in every case the divine and supernatural truth

This being said, it must be acknowledged that the attempt to ascertain which is the genuine and original Greek text according to tradition in the Orthodox Church, and the publication of an edition of the New Testament embodying such a text, is fraught with difficulties. This is especially so inasmuch as there exist several families and categories of different classes of manuscripts, on which most of the editions have been based, without any one of them being adjudged entirely accurate, complete, and perfect.

There also exist in our Eastern Church, on a somewhat more official level, editions issued by the local Orthodox Churches, such as (among others) the edition brought out in 1903 by the Ecumenical Patriarchate. This 'did not have the same aim as the so-called critical editions, that is, the discovery and restoration of the original text of the sacred books; but its aim was simply to restore the most ancient text—without taking into account the more recently printed editions —as found in the ecclesiastical tradition, and most notably in that of the Church of Constantinople'. Such also was the aim of the Slavonic translation of the New Testament and of the Slavonic editions of this translation issued from time to time: these show a striking similarity to the prevailing text in the Greek ecclesiastical tradition. Not that this whole question can in any way be considered as settled and thoroughly investigated and clarified. Thus our Holy Orthodox Church should entrust to expert Orthodox theologians the task of editing the best possible scholarly edition of the original Greek text of the New Testament, so that the text so prepared may thereafter be recognized and accepted by the whole of our Holy Orthodox Church.

# V  SACRED TRADITION

*The Definition of its Meaning*

As regards the vast and fundamental subject of Sacred Tradition, which is the other means whereby the one and unique Revelation of God expresses itself, our Holy Orthodox Church provides the following definition of it: Sacred Tradition is the teaching of our Lord and the Apostles, transmitted orally by them and handed down in live speech by the Church, which has also been written down in the Church, through the action of the Holy Spirit. With the passage of time and under the guidance of the Church's shepherds, the successors of the Apostles who have borne the responsibility for rightly proclaiming the word of truth, this teaching has become articulated into the catholic mind and the unified conscience of the Church, which in itself, and also in virtue of its apostolic succession from the Apostles, possesses the criterion of its own truth: and for this reason it is known as 'apostolic truth' and 'apostolic mind'. Following this it was interpreted, treasured up, and embodied in specific forms with the passage of time: in the ancient creeds, the doctrinal definitions and creeds of the Holy Councils, especially those that were Ecumenical, in the authentic interpretations of Holy Scripture by the Church, and also in the worship, the universally prevailing customs and the general practice of the Church as a whole. Finally, this doctrine was taken up and expanded—through the faithful and correct interpretation of the elements handed down—in the various writings, notably dogmatic, polemic and apologetic, of the Fathers and other Doctors of the Church, over a period of many centuries. Thus it emerged as Holy (or Sacred) Tradition, in the broad sense of the term. As such, in its entirety, it is the other bearer of divine revelation, concordant with and equal in authority to Holy Scripture in the One, Holy, Catholic and Apostolic Church.

From the above it appears beyond dispute that Scripture was preceded by this original 'oral tradition', the 'form of doctrine' (Rom. 6.17—NEB: 'pattern of teaching'), the 'canon' of faith and teaching (2 Cor. 10.13, 15, 16), the 'truth which has been entrusted' (1 Tim. 6.20 and 2 Tim. 1.14), the 'Gospel of salvation' (Eph. 1.13) which the Apostles and their immediate associates preached and by preaching handed down to following generations, as St Paul says: 'But what matter, I or they? This is what we all proclaim, and this is what you believed' (1 Cor. 15.11), 'either by word or by letter'. He considers these teachings as 'traditions', to which we are exhorted to 'hold fast' (2 Thess. 2.15). From this first tradition the content of the New Testament was formed without, of course, exhausting the whole of oral tradition. Again, this oral tradition did not render Holy Scripture superfluous and unnecessary as a form of Divine Revelation, but after the formation of the sacred texts it continued to fulfil the same role as before: it was the teaching that was preached by our Lord and His Apostles, the truth learnt 'by hearsay' (Rom. 10.17) and formed into the living conscience in the Church.

Strictly speaking, Scripture never superseded Tradition, but both remained equal bearers of the divine Revelation, equally important forms of its expression, with this difference: Scripture, completed and fully formed, as we have already noted, at a given moment of time in the Church, composed the canon of the New Testament in its final and definitive state; while Tradition, passed on orally and preserved by hearsay in the Church, moved through a variety of formative channels, but always remained faithful, under the guidance of the Paraclete, to Him who leads the Church 'into all truth' (John 16.13); it is contained in the ecclesiastical texts already mentioned, and so it comes to constitute Sacred Tradition.

## 1. APOSTOLIC AND ECCLESIASTICAL TRADITION

Viewed in this way, chronologically, Sacred Tradition can be divided into two parts: Apostolic Tradition and Ecclesiastical Tradition. Ecclesiastical Tradition stems from the Apostolic and perpetuates it, being its continuation.

On the one hand, Apostolic Tradition is at the same time ecclesiastical, since it is lived within the Church and has crystallized under specific conditions within the historical reality of the Church. On the other hand, Ecclesiastical Tradition is related directly or indirectly to the apostolic truth, being always in agreement with the teaching of Scripture, which it interprets and develops, and constituting its broadest and most practical application in Church life, thus facilitating the comprehension, in its fullest sense, of the saving truth of God.

As such, Sacred Tradition is itself a source and mode of expression of Revelation, as also is Holy Scripture. The components forming Sacred Tradition require to be carefully preserved, accurately interpreted, and rightly expressed through the Holy Spirit within the Church; they are then treasured up by the Fathers and teachers of the Church in written sources and records, without losing in the course of this process any of the marks of their 'apostolicity'. They are then regarded in the Church as constituting definitively, along

9

with Holy Scripture, the second source or, to express it differently, as being equal in honour to Scripture as a form of expression of the divine Revelation given through Jesus Christ in the Holy Spirit.

It is just such a notion of Tradition, in its broad unfolding and development, that St Athanasius has in mind when he says: 'From the beginning there has been one *tradition* and *doctrine* and *faith* of the catholic Church, which the Lord gave, the Apostles preached, and the Fathers preserved. It is on this that the Church is grounded'.[1] It is the Church's responsibility throughout the ages to 'guard it jealously' and to 'pass it on with common consent'. In so doing, the Church maintains and guards intact and alive the word of God entrusted to her and, though scattered and dispersed throughout the world, she thus ensures her own cohesion and contact with the original source of the word and Revelation: with the Lord. 'Having received this preaching and this faith, the Church, albeit scattered throughout the world, guards them carefully, as though dwelling in one house: and likewise she believes in these things, as though having one soul and the same heart, and with common consent she teaches and hands them down as if possessing but one mouth. For though the elect throughout the world are dissimilar, yet the *strength of the tradition* is one and the same'.[2]

In Tradition thus delineated, certain marks stand out with regard to the notion of 'passing on' or 'transmitting', which is the basic principle of the living Tradition within the living Church of the ever-living Christ.

## 2. 'PASSING ON' THE TEACHING IN SACRED TRADITION

Who is the 'passer on' (*ho paradidôn*) in the transmission of the one revealed truth? Since the very beginning there has existed in the Church's conscience the conviction that the chief persons in the realm of Tradition are linked in one and the same supernatural chain, and that this chain, proceeding from and passing through the Lord and His Apostles, reaches as far as the bishops and other ministers of the word and the sacraments living in different districts and cities. This truth is voiced by Clement of Rome, when he says: 'The Apostles proclaimed the good news to us from the Lord Jesus Christ; Jesus Christ was sent from God. Christ came therefore from God, and the Apostles from Christ. Thus both came in the appointed order from the will of God. Having received a charge and having been fully assured through the resurrection of our Lord Jesus Christ, and having been confirmed in the word of God with the full assurance of the Holy Spirit, they went forth proclaiming that the Kingdom of God was at hand. Preaching in the country and in the towns, and baptizing all who bowed to the will of God, they raised up their first-fruits—having tried them in the Spirit—as bishops and deacons[3] for those who should believe. Nor was this a novelty: for bishops and deacons had been written about from very ancient times. Thus scripture says: "I shall establish their bishops in righteousness and their deacons in faith" '.[4]

So, with regard to the person or persons 'passing on' the teaching in Sacred Tradition, we have as a closely established principle that, just as the doctrine expounded by the various persons mentioned above is linked by upward ascent through the Apostles and the Lord, to the God of all Himself; so this teaching, proceeding from God, is continued throughout the ages, without any doubt or deviation, by downward descent through the same persons. In this manner Sacred Tradition is established, from the viewpoint of those persons who pass it on, as a reality ever-living within the Church, yet never in any way altered.

As for the substance of what is passed on in Sacred Tradition, the historical sources of the Church call it by different names: 'didascalia', 'didache', 'kerygma', 'logos' or 'logoi' or 'logia' (meaning 'teaching', 'preaching', 'sayings'), 'commandments of God and the Lord' and especially 'evangelion(-lia)'—'gospel(s)' or 'good news'. Thus Justin the Apologist says, 'The Apostles, in their records known as gospels, thus passed on the message entrusted to them'.[5] These are all synonymous with the 'traditions' (*paradoseis*) mentioned by the Apostolic and other Fathers, and they are identical with the basic teachings of the Apostles, since 'just as the teaching of all the apostles was one, so also is their tradition.'[6] 'The teaching', so it has been said, 'was passed on in this way from the Apostles through their lawful successors, and it has continued to exist in the Churches up to this very day; and so nothing else should be accepted save that which in no way conflicts with the tradition of the Church and the Apostles'.[7]

Subsequent Fathers of the Church proceeded to specify further the nature of 'what has been passed on' (*paradedomenon*). So the historian Eusebius states precisely that the Lord's disciples 'handed over for preservation some things in writing and others by means of unwritten ordinances',[8] while St Athanasius, speaking from his own personal viewpoint specifically about the 'gospel tradition' and 'apostolic tradition', says that it constitutes the entire orthodox teaching of the Church, through which 'we believe as a result in the gospel and apostolic tradition'.[9]

Three facts, then, emerge with regard to the act of transmission within Sacred Tradition: (a) the existence of the Lord's saving teaching, passed on by the Apostles, (b) its preservation in the Church, and (c) its subsequent transmission to those who come after.

In Sacred Tradition, everything 'being passed on' (paradidomenon) is necessarily linked with the supernatural truth revealed by the Lord, linked, too, with the Apostles and their immediate associates and successors. A wider factor that is directly involved is the Paraclete, present in the Church: for it is in His name and through His grace that there takes place every act of fresh transmission and handing down of the revealed truth and ecclesiastical doctrine.

'. . . None will adjudge these things save the Holy Spirit passed on in the Church, which the Apostles were the first to receive, and then they passed it on to those who had believed aright. We, being their successors and partakers of the same grace, high priesthood and teaching, and being reckoned as guardians of the Church, will not slumber or keep silent from voicing the word of truth; nor will we grow weary in body and soul as we struggle to give back worthy fruits to God our benefactor, without thereby repaying Him as He deserves. Yet we shall not act carelessly in the things entrusted to us, but we shall act with due measure as each situation requires and share in every gift which the Holy Spirit bestows abundantly upon all. Not only have we brought to light and passed judgement on what is amiss, but also whatever the Truth has received from the grace of the Father and dispensed to men; these things we have noted by our words and witnessed to them in our writings, and we preach them unashamed'.[10]

This passage from Hippolytus brings us already to another question: To whom are the things passed on in Tradition entrusted? Undoubtedly they are entrusted—from an immediate and narrow point of view—to the direct successors of the Apostles and the pastors of the Church who succeeded them, the bishops; then, from a wider viewpoint, they are entrusted to all the priestly orders in the Church, irrespective of rank, from the presbyter down to the catechist; finally, in a still wider ecclesiological context, they are entrusted to the whole fulness (pleroma) of the Church, to the faithful as a whole. It is the faithful as a whole who are at once the objects and the subjects of this Sacred Tradition operative in the Church:

objects, inasmuch as Sacred Tradition, along with Holy Scripture —that is, the whole of Revelation—has as its goal their life in Christ and their salvation; subjects, because it is chiefly they who, by their acceptance in faith and by the witness of their conscience, contribute towards the perfect preservation of this received truth and teaching and towards its fresh transmission, undiminished, to future generations.

*Extent of Sacred Tradition*
In Sacred Tradition, as an ever-living reality within the Church, as also in Holy Scripture, there are to be found together three basic and fundamental elements, closely joined in unity in the supernatural fact of Divine Revelation. These are: (1) the divine and supernatural element, this being the primary factor; (2) the ecclesiastical element, which constitutes Sacred Tradition as an outward form of Revelation and as the fully articulated teaching of the Church: this exists as a reality within the Church alone, and through the Church it is made the possession of the faithful who are called to salvation; (3) the outward or human element which not only gives to Sacred Tradition its human dimension, but helps us to understand how and why God, speaking to men 'in fragmentary and varied fashion' in Revelation in general, has made use of all kinds of human methods and forms —of different persons and institutions, of various types of written records and living experiences; and this He has done, not only in order to transmit the revealed truth through the ages, but also in order to give to the saving Tradition of the Church a specific shape and structure.

With regard to the divine factor in Sacred Tradition, the most striking feature is its theocentric character. Without this divine and supernatural factor it is impossible to conceive of either Divine Revelation in itself nor, by extension and analogy, of Sacred Tradition.

Viewed in this theocentric perspective, Sacred Tradition is seen to possess a Trinitarian character. The Father through the Son in the Holy Spirit spoke to mankind in the whole Revelation. The Father through the Son in the Holy Spirit is He who perpetuates among men the saving truth and teaching, and who preserves it secure, entire and intact, within the Church, thereby making evident the divine-human nature of Tradition.

From this, two fundamental points follow of themselves: (*a*) there is but one divine revelation alike in Holy Scripture and in Sacred

13

Tradition, both being derived from the one God of all; (*b*) since the present discussion is concerned more particularly with the sufficiency of these two things, it must be emphasized from our Orthodox standpoint that divine revelation is not exhausted either by Scripture alone or by Tradition alone, but only by Scripture in Tradition, and that both together constitute the plenitude of the divine revelation in Christ Jesus.

For the Church, the important thing has not been the outward form or the mode of expression of the revealed truth, but the truth *itself*. That is why the same Fathers defended the revealed truth in Christ, both that in Scripture and that handed down in Tradition, in such a way as to underline the parallel character of both, not as two circles touching, but as concentric, with the same self-revealing God for their centre.

It is of course true that, immediately after the fixing of the canon of Holy Scripture, it was thought in the Church that Scripture contained all the saving truths of faith. This question has been sufficiently dealt with above. There are many texts in the leading Fathers both of East and West (the Apologists, Irenaeus, Tertullian, Clement of Alexandria, Origen, Cyprian, Athanasius, Cyril of Jerusalem, Jerome, Cyril of Alexandria, Augustine, etc.), which emphasize the 'sufficiency' of Holy Scripture, as containing all the truths necessary for man's salvation. However, these Fathers also stressed the distinctive contribution of Tradition, taken as a whole, to this sufficiency of Scripture, and they insist that 'it is only when examined in the light of Sacred Tradition that Scripture shines forth as the sufficient and complete treasure-house of Christian truths. It was from this standpoint that the Church Fathers, who otherwise extolled Tradition as a source equal in value to Scripture, . . . described Scripture as the complete code of doctrines; these, in connection with Tradition, were understood as scriptural teachings and proceeded, based on Tradition through analysis or otherwise, from Scripture'.

Yet on the other hand it is equally known that this 'sufficiency' should in no way be taken to mean, in an absolute sense, that Scripture alone can be considered to contain and embrace the whole of Revelation. Such an extreme view is as erroneous as the opinion at the opposite extreme, that Tradition alone embraces the whole of divine revelation, and that from it, both chronologically and quantitively, there proceeds—as a dependent derivative—Holy Scripture.

Taking into account this close-knit relationship between Tradition and Scripture, the living Tradition may be said to have preceded

Scripture in so far as the oral word, the oral form of teaching, preceded the handing-down in writing of the revealed truth, 'but it cannot be said that Tradition was drawn from Scripture, nor that Scripture fully exhausted Tradition'. Without Holy Scripture, regarded as the most ancient embodiment of the gospel, the Christian teaching could not have been preserved in all its purity. On the other hand, without exact Tradition we should not be able to grasp the deep meaning of the Scriptures, nor would we even have the Scriptures. Tradition and Scripture make up one single whole.

Our Holy Orthodox Church starts from the principle that—as St Athanasius says—truly 'the holy and divinely-inspired scriptures are sufficient for the exposition of the truth'.[11] But our Church in no way rejects the teaching, that alongside these scriptures (to quote St Athanasius once more), 'there are also many treatises composed on these themes by our blessed teachers; and if anyone reads them, he will gain some notion of the interpretation of the scriptures'.[12] She also acknowledges that, 'of the dogmas and preaching preserved in the Church, some we have through written teaching, while others have been handed down to us secretly from the tradition of the Apostles; both, however, are equal in authority . . .'.[13] Our Church thus believes, together with St John Chrysostom, that 'not all things were handed down in writing, but many were transmitted in unwritten form; but both the former and the latter are deserving of credence, so that we regard the tradition of the Church as worthy of belief';[14] and that, in the words of St Epiphanius, 'one should also make use of tradition; for it is not always possible to obtain everything from holy scripture; that is why the holy apostles handed down some things in writing, and others in tradition'.[15] That is why our Holy Orthodox Church not only teaches that Scripture and Tradition are equal in authority and on an equal footing—as we have already said very many times—but also acknowledges that divine revelation and the infallible teaching of the Church that accords with it are not expressed one-sidedly by 'Scripture alone', nor, again, in isolation by 'Tradition alone', but by 'Scripture and Tradition': Scripture is understood within Tradition, while Tradition preserves its own purity and the criterion of its own truth through Scripture and the contents of Scripture.

3. The ecclesiastical factor in Sacred Tradition
The Church's formulation of revealed truths

With regard to the ecclesiastical factor in Tradition, this brings us at once to the many-sided ecclesiological dimension of Tradition. In particular, it is immediately evident that Tradition cannot be considered apart from its natural setting within the Church as a divine-human institution. Indeed, Tradition is not only one facet of the general work of God, acting *ad extra* in revelation, but also a sort of supernatural ministry within the world, a ministry which by its very nature and status presupposes the institution and personal members of the Church, in order to express itself in a concrete form as a channel of revealed truth and thereby of saving faith and teaching among men.

This entails defining two things: the Church's method of formulating revealed truths, and the valid witness within the Church provided by her common conscience concerning true teaching.

Our Holy Orthodox Church, with regard to the first point, maintains that the definition and formulation of the truths contained in Holy Scripture and Sacred Tradition can be performed by the Church, and by her alone, through bishops gathered in a Council. For it is to them that the Apostles entrusted the word of God; it is they who, as successors to the Apostles, are linked by them to the One Lord Christ, who is in the primary and strict sense the bearer of divine revelation. They are not to be considered in isolation, simply as the spiritual heads of the large or small flock entrusted to their pastoral oversight. For beyond the narrow confines of their administrative jurisdiction, they have a greater responsibility in the Church at large, seeing that, as St John Chrysostom says, 'He who has charge of a local Church should not only keep watch over that Church which the Spirit has placed in his hands, but over the Church throughout the world . . .'.[16] They are to be considered not as individuals but primarily as a body—as together comprising the sacred order of the episcopate, assembled in the same place and through the Holy Spirit expressing their judgement in council on themes of faith and truth.

This dual ecclesiological role brings to the fore two basic principles of ecclesiology that are linked with Tradition: firstly, the Apostolic Succession, and secondly, the Church's practice of meeting and voicing her view through the bishops in a council.

## 4. The Apostolic Succession, the institution of the Council and Sacred Tradition

It follows incontrovertibly from the above that the Apostolic Succession is a basic factor in Tradition. It is no exaggeration to say that, without the Apostolic Succession in the Church there is no true and unerring Tradition, for the simple reason that, without a succession of persons, there is no unbroken succession of grace or teaching; it is only in both, in the succession of persons and teaching, that the revealed truth is seen to be preserved and handed down through the ages, faithfully and integrally.

At the same time, Tradition is closely bound up with the institution of the Council, whereby the Church comes together and voices its opinion through its bishops; for the Apostolic Succession in the strict sense, which we have mentioned above as a presupposition of Tradition, is an institution founded directly on the hierarchy, on the bishops, as successors of the Apostles to whom they trace their origin; and it is they who maintain the continuity, unity and sameness of the revealed doctrine and Tradition.

This is stated concisely in the ancient Holy Tradition by Hegesippus and Irenaeus. Hegesippus says: 'In every succession and in every city, that which the law and the prophets and the Lord preach is faithfully followed',[17] while Irenaeus says: '. . . It is by the same order and the same teaching, that the tradition of the Apostles in the Church and the preaching of the truth have reached us'.[18] In more recent times the same has been said by Peter Moghila in his *Confession* when he emphasizes that the bishops 'after their ordination possess both the unbroken succession and the power to teach the saving dogmas, for this is the task for which they are sent'.[19]

That the bishops should come together and voice their opinions in harmony in a Council is as essential for Tradition as is the conciliar system itself for the Church. As a result, we often see the Fathers stressing this reality of the conciliar decision of the Church's bishops; and it is emphasized not only in an ecclesiological sense, but also in connection with the chief characteristic of the Church as an institution preserving and perpetuating the revealed truth in Tradition and its teaching. Thus we find St John Chrysostom saying that 'no (bishop) is able to do anything of himself', and that '(the bishops) become more venerable through the synod and their great numbers',[20] while Cyril of Alexandria observes succinctly that 'on theological and ecclesiastical issues, it is the will of the holy fathers and the synod that prevails'.[21]

## 5. The common conscience of the Church and Sacred Tradition

Concerning the witness of the faithful, otherwise known as the common conscience of the Church, our Holy Orthodox Church acknowledges that the link between Sacred Tradition and the Church's common conscience, in which truth is lived by the pleroma, is extremely close and real. It is true that all authority in the Church has as its source and its support the system whereby the Church expresses itself and reaches decisions on matters of faith and life in Christ through the bishops gathered in an Ecumenical Council. Yet this authority is not to be conceived apart from the common conscience of the Church, which must accompany it. This 'common conscience' is the unanimous joint opinion of clergy and laity, that is to say, the witness of the whole pleroma of the Church; and so it should not be regarded as in some way different from, foreign to, or independent of the Church as it makes official pronouncements. Rather, it is a witness joined with it, testifying to the same revealed truth and the same teaching, believed in identically; so that it is not possible to conceive of ecclesiastical authority apart from the broader witness borne by the common conscience of the Church's pleroma, nor, on the other hand, to conceive of a common conscience apart from the Church as authoritatively teaching the facts of faith. That is how we should envisage the true functioning of the common conscience in the one undivided Church of the great holy Ecumenical Councils. As history shows, it has always supported unreservedly all the teachings and definitions drawn up in these Councils through the Holy Spirit, and it has always rebelled against those assemblies which deviated from the truth; for the common conscience of the Church acted as a watchdog, ever-ready to accept all truth correctly expounded and properly defined, and to pounce on any deviation from the truth that was treasured up in the Church and in Tradition.

It is self-evident that Sacred Tradition is not an artificial accumulation of ideas, joined to each other merely by external links, but an inner body of truths proceeding from God, transmitted in living fashion in the Church, and formulated, so far as its human aspect is concerned, under the inspiration and the grace of the Holy Spirit. In the same way, the Church's common conscience is not merely an artificial creation contrived by the Church's members in obedience to instructions or dictation from above, but the natural fruit of the teaching and preaching ministry carried out by the pastors of the Church under the Spirit's guidance. The grace of the Spirit leads the inner man to knowledge, understanding and faith in the truths revealed, in accordance with its role within the Church, which is to guide men 'into all truth' (John 16.13), in order that the faithful, being of the same mind, may make up one body under one head—the one Lord God.

From this it follows that the common conscience of the Church is a quality not met with in each and every member separately, but formed and developed within the body of the Church as a whole. Just as Tradition is a universal reality in virtue of the divine revelation treasured up within the Church, so the common conscience is a universal ministry within the Church, for it is the witness of the entire body of the faithful concerning the content of Tradition and the teaching of the Church.

### 6. THE HUMAN OR EXTERNAL FACTOR IN SACRED TRADITION

Finally, with regard to the human, or external, factor in Tradition, this not only confers upon it its anthropological dimension, but also explains why God made special use of such human means and devices as people, institutions and various types of written records and living experiences within the Church, contributing to the transmission and handing-down of revealed truth and its gradual shaping into fully articulated ecclesiastical truth, in the recognized forms of Tradition in the Church.

Man, as at once the subject and the object in the entire functioning of Tradition, is undoubtedly the one through whom and for whom Tradition exists, and indeed the one who, under the Church's guidance, plays a decisive role in it, both in its human shaping and expression, and in its further evolution and transmission from person to person.

In this context, Vincent of Lérins gives an excellent description and analysis of this anthropological dimension of Sacred Tradition, saying briefly: 'Moreover, in the Catholic Church all possible care must be taken that we hold that faith which has been believed everywhere, always, and by all: for that is truly and in the strictest sense catholic. . . . And this will come about if we follow universality, antiquity and agreement'.[22]

Here, then, Vincent stresses three fundamental characteristics: universality, antiquity, and unanimous agreement, all three of which naturally presuppose the existence of the human element.

### 7. THE CONCRETE EXTERNAL FORMS TAKEN BY
### SACRED TRADITION IN THE CHURCH

That which was believed everywhere, always, and by all in the Church assumed specific forms for its external manifestation and human expression and definition, which can be listed as follows: (*a*) The official formulations and confessions of faith of the ancient Church; (*b*) The definitions, creeds and canons of the Ecumenical Councils and the decisions and canons of local councils confirmed by them and the Fathers; (*c*) Valid and authentic interpretations of Scripture; (*d*) Texts used in worship and, above all, the Divine Liturgy, and (*e*) The agreed teaching of the Church Fathers ('consensus Patrum').

All these forms together constitute the clear expression of the Church's faith and doctrine. The official formulations and confessions of faith of the ancient Church 'contain in a few lines the whole doctrine of faith . . .'.[23] The definitions, creeds, and canons of the Ecumenical Councils set out categorically and authentically that which 'the catholic Church believes' and which the God-inspired Fathers 'at once confessed they believed, so as to show that their way of thinking as they wrote was not new-fangled but apostolic, not invented by them but what the Apostles had taught'.[24] The valid and authentic interpretations of Scripture establish in what way 'the divine canon of Scripture is interpreted according to the traditions of the Catholic Church and in accordance with catholic doctrine'.[25] The texts used in worship and the Divine Liturgy provide a comprehensive and substantial form of the faith of the Catholic Church as confessed by her in worship, according to the well-known law, 'lex orandi lex credendi'. The agreed teaching of the Fathers is the voice of the ever-living faith and teaching of the Church, since they 'followed the will of Scripture',[26] 'through the Holy Spirit . . . pastors and teachers have spoken',[27] becoming, through their agreement over a narrower or wider field, the interpreters and continuers of revealed truth and of Tradition down the ages.

'The word of God is not bound', says St Paul (2 Tim. 2.9). Such is the character of God's Revelation. Perfected in the Son, it was treasured up by the Apostles in the Church, to be kept by her in purity, correctly interpreted, fully believed, and accurately taught, and as such spread throughout the world, that all who receive it 'may not be lost but have eternal life', and that through it men may come to know 'thee who alone art truly God, and Jesus Christ whom thou hast sent' (John 17.3).

NOTES

1. *Letter to Serapion*, 28, P.G. 26, 539.
2. St Irenaeus, *Against false knowledge*, 10, 2.
3. This means presbyters as well.

4. .Clement of Rome, *Epistle to the Corinthians,* I, 42, cf. *Phil..* 1.1 *and Didache,* 2; Polycarp of Smyrna, *To the Philippians,* 1.2; Ignatius of Antioch, *To the Magnesians,* 6.1 and 13.1, *To the Trallians,* 2.2.

5. Justin, *Apologia I,* 66, 3.

6. Clement of Alexandria, *Stromateis,* VII,17.

7. Origen, *On First Principles,* I, Preface, 2, P.G. 11, 116, cf. *Homilies* 39 and 46 on Matthew, P.G. 13, 1656 and 1667.

8. Eusebius, *Gospel Proofs,* 1, 8, P.G. 22, 76.

9. Athanasius, *Against Apollinarius,* Sermon 1, 2, P.G. 26, 1132; *To Adelphius,* 6, P.G. 26, 1080 and *On the Events at Ariminum,* 23, P.G. 26, 721. Cf. Cyril of Jerusalem, *Mystag. Catecheses,* v. 11 and v. 5, P.G. 33, 1117, also Cyril of Alexandria, *On the Orthodox Faith,* 3, P.G. 76, 1264.

10. Hippolytus, *A Judgement on all Heresies,* Prologue.

11. Athanasius, *Against the Greeks,* 1, 3, P.G. 25, 4.

12. Athanasius, ibid.

13. St Basil, *On the Holy Spirit,* 26, 61, P.G. 32, 188.

14. Chrysostom, *On II Thess.,* Homily 4, 2, P.G. 62, 488.

15. Epiphanius, Panarion, *Against Heresies* 61, 6, P.G. 41, 1048. Cf. also Gregory of Nyssa, *Against Eunomius,* 32, P.G. 22, 672; Cyril of Alex., *That Christ is one,* Dialogue in question and answer form, P.G. 75, 1257; Gregory Nazianzen, Letter 101, P.G. 37, 176; John of Damascus, *Sermon on Holy Icons,* 2, 28, P.G. 94, 1312–17; Pseudo-Dionysius, *On the Ecclesiastical Hierarchy,* 1, 4, P.G. 3, 375.

16. Chrysostom, *On St Eustathios,* 3, P.G. 50, 602.

17. Fragm. 5, in *Eusebius,* 4, 22, 3.

18. *Against Heresies,* III, 3, 3.

19. J. Karmiris, *Dogmatic and Symbolic Records,* II, Athens 1953, p. 640.

20. Chrysostom, *Homilies on Acts,* 37, 3, P.G. 60, 266.

21. Cyril of Alex., Letter 17, P.G. 77, 108.

22. *Commonitorium,* 2, P.L. 50, 630.

23. Cyril of Jerusalem, *Catechesis* V, 12, P.G. 33, 520–21.

24. St Athanasius, *That the Council at Nicaea* . . . 3 and 27, P.G. 25, 420 and 465; *On the Council of Ariminum,* 5, P.G. 26, 688.

25. Vincent of Lérins, *Commonitorium* 2, 27, P.L. 50, 675.

26. St Basil, *On the Holy Spirit,* 7, P.G. 32, 96.

27. John of Damascus, *Exposition of the Orthodox Faith,* 4, 17, P.G. 94, 1176.

# 2

## Fuller participation by the laity in the worship and life of the Church

On the theme, 'Fuller Participation by the Laity in the Worship and Life of the Church', the Interorthodox Preparatory Commission reports as follows:

The dogmatic and canonical teaching of our Holy Orthodox Church is clear on this point. The laity, together with the clergy, makes up the Body of Christ (Rom. 12.5, 1 Cor. 12.27, Eph. 5.30), the People of God (Matt. 1.21, 2.6, 2 Cor. 7.16 cf. Heb. 10.30, 11.25, Apoc. 18.4, 21.3), a royal priesthood (1 Pet. 2.9). In the visible Church, however, there have been instituted shepherds and sheep (Acts 20.28, 1 Pet. 5.2, Eph. 11.12). The Church on earth consists of two orders, clergy and laity, inasmuch as 'the appointed order in the Churches has established, on the one hand, the flock and, on the other, shepherds' (Gregory of Nazianzus, P.G. 36, 185). United and inseparable, both these orders are essential and necessary components of the Church. The first order, that of the shepherds, consists of the ecclesiastical hierarchy constituted and existing in the Church by the divine will through the sacrament of ordination; the second order consists of the flock that bears Christ's name, established in the Church through the sacraments of Baptism and Chrismation (Confirmation). The two orders of clergy and laity constitute together the one indivisible body of Christ, the one and undivided Church. All alike, both clergy and laity, are participants in the sacrament of Baptism, which incorporates them into one and the same body, the Church; all alike participate in the sacrament of the Eucharist and in all the gifts of the Holy Spirit granted in the Church through the sacraments and in other ways. The clergy are distinguished from the laity by the sacramental priesthood which they received at their ordination, transmitted by the unbroken apostolic succession of the bishops as bearers of the truth of the apostolic tradition. Each of these two essential components of the Church's Body has special and distinctive rights and duties within it; all suppression or confusion of the special rights and duties of each is excluded, as well as mutual interference. Both are 'one in the Lord, some leading the way to what is right, others following in the same spirit . . .' (St Basil, P.G. 32, 820).

Thus the nature of lay participation in the life of the Church is clearly expressed in her dogmatic and canonical teaching; it is not a question causing special concern to the Orthodox Church and, for the time being at any rate, it does not constitute a burning problem for her. In all conscience the Orthodox Church believes that there has never been, nor is there now, a spontaneous movement among the laity to acquire greater rights and duties in the Church, different from those which they have had since the Church's foundation. For they have always participated actively in worship and administration, in the pastoral work and teaching ministry of the Church, according to the rights and duties clearly laid upon them by Holy Tradition and the Canons. Their main rights and duties, as lay people and members of the Church, are to live in the fullness of the gifts of divine grace within our Holy Church and to witness by word and way of life to Christ the Saviour and to His gospel.

# 3

## *Adaptation of the ecclesiastical ordinances regarding fasting to meet present-day needs*

Fasting is a very ancient practice, found in nearly all nations throughout the ages. People fasted to show sorrow or to prepare for great religious festivals, when they prayed and called down grace from on high. As a religious and sacramental institution in pre-Christian religions, it not only had a religious purpose, such as the purification of the soul, but also aimed at bodily hygiene, inasmuch as the priests of some religions were at the same time doctors (as in Egypt, for example). In ancient Greece fasting, along with other practices, was regarded as a means of atonement and purification prior to approaching the gods, while through fasting the Romans honoured Ceres and Jupiter.

In the beginning, the Mosaic law imposed only one national fast each year on the Jews; it lasted for a single day, the Day of Atonement, and was an expression of humility: '. . . And this shall be a statute for ever unto you: that in the seventh month, on the tenth day of the month, ye shall humiliate your souls. . . . It shall be a sabbath of rest unto you, and ye shall humiliate your souls, by a statute for ever' (Lev. 16.29 and 31; cf. 23.27). After the captivity, however, the number of fast days among the Jews increased, in memory of national misfortunes and other events in their history: 'Blow a trumpet in Zion, sanctify a fast, call a solemn assembly. . . . Spare thy people, O Lord, and give not thine heritage to reproach, that the heathen should rule over them . . .' (Joel 2.15 and 17; cf. Jonah 3.5–8 *et al.*). During their fasts the Jews showed repentance by eating little and late, and by subjecting themselves to various other privations.

In our Lord's time, the Jews observed the fasts, and none more strictly than the Pharisees, who fasted twice in the week, on Monday and on Thursday (Luke 18.12). Jesus Christ did not abolish fasting but hallowed it, fasting Himself for forty days in the wilderness before beginning His public work (Matt. 4.1–2). He gave instructions to His disciples on how they were to fast, bitterly condemning the hypocrisy of the Pharisees which revealed itself during the fasts: 'Moreover when ye fast, be not, as the hypocrites, of a sad countenance: for they disfigure their faces, that they may appear unto men to fast. Verily I say unto you, they have their reward. But thou, when thou fastest, anoint thine head, and wash thy face; that thou appear not unto men to fast, but unto thy Father which is in secret: and thy Father, which seeth in secret, shall reward thee openly' (Matt. 6.16–18). In many places throughout the New Testament fasting is recommended as a means of temperance, spiritual exaltation, and repentance (Acts 9.9, 13.2, 14.23, 1 Cor. 7.5).

As a result, fasting became a hallowed custom also in the Church. At first, Christians observed the Jewish fasts of Monday and Thursday. Later on, by way of contrast, Wednesday and Friday were appointed as fast days: 'Let not your fasts be with the hypocrites: whereas they fast each week on Mondays and Thursdays, you should fast on the fourth day of the week and on Friday.[1] Nevertheless the spirit of freedom reigned at that time regarding the observance of the fast.[2] There was no fixed rule for the time or manner of fasting before Easter: 'Some think that they should fast for one day, others for two, others still more, while in the opinion of others, the "day" amounts to forty continuous hours'.[3] At the beginning of the 3rd century, Tertullian mentions a two-day fast, on Friday and Saturday (*De jejunio*, 14). Christians observed a complete fast until evening, while some did not even break their fast with an evening meal, but continued it uninterruptedly for two days. Prolongation of the fast beyond the evening of the same day was called 'hyperthesis', Latin 'superpositio', but was always a matter of free choice. The fast preceding Easter was extended to last for at least a week during the first half of the third century. Dionysius of Alexandria (250) speaks of such a fast. Hyperthesis was extended at the same time. Some observed it throughout the whole of Holy Week, others for fewer days, say four or three or two, while on other days they kept the usual fast, that is, until evening. There were Christians who, throughout Holy Week, kept a fast only until evening, without hyperthesis: 'for not all of them observed all six of the fast days to the same degree; some remain without food, practising hyperthesis, for all of them, while others do so for only two, three, or four days, and some not at all'.[4] Other writers describe the foodstuffs consumed in the evening by those Christians who did not observe hyperthesis. Epiphanius

25

(403) mentions xerophagia, or dry foods, meaning bread, salt, and water (*On Faith*, 22.10). The Apostolic Constitutions (fourth century) include vegetables as well as these foods (5.18). The pre-Easter fast was later extended to forty days; the 5th Canon of the 1st Ecumenical Council (325) mentions such a fast in passing as something already in existence. This prolongation was first introduced into the Church during the terrible persecution of the Emperors Galerius, Maximin, and Licinius (306–323), following the example of Jesus Christ, Moses, and Elijah.[5] The practice had already emerged during the second half of the third century among ascetics and others leading a life of self-denial, who before Easter observed a forty-day fast. The Christians who fled from the cities on account of persecution came to places where the ascetics lived, and copied them. The fast of forty days was not immediately adopted everywhere. In some places, at any rate, there were intermediate stages, with a fast ranging from two to three weeks. Sozomen (fifth century) says: 'Some fast for three weeks, spread out over a six or seven week period; others fast continuously for three weeks immediately before the feast; others only for two, such as the followers of Montanus'.[6] In the subsequent period as well, there existed different practices in different Churches concerning the length of the Easter fast, some keeping a six-week and others a seven-week fast. That of seven weeks was customary in Constantinople, Thrace, Asia Minor, and Syria (excluding Palestine), while all other regions had a six-week fast. 'As for the 40-day fast, some put it at six weeks, such as the Illyrians and the tribes to the West, the whole of Libya and Egypt along with the people of Palestine, while others count seven weeks, as in Constantinople and the surrounding tribes as far as the Phoenicians'.[7] After the fifth century certain regions that had the six-week fast joined the other party. These regions were Palestine, Egypt and Eastern Illyricum. Thus there persisted a difference in the duration of the Easter fast between the Eastern and the Western part of the Church.

From the seventh century on, there was added in the Eastern Church the 'week of cheese-fare', which previously was to be found only sporadically. The form of the Holy Week fast remained the same as described above.[8] On the other weeks there is plenty of information. The historian Socrates (fifth century) says that there was no written rule on the subject and that a wide variety of customs prevailed regarding the fast. Some ate only dry bread, while others ate fruit and eggs, others fish, and some poultry. Socrates praises and recommends this freedom. 'Some abstain altogether from living things, others partake only of fish from amongst living things, while others eat poultry as well as fish, saying that according to Moses these too have come from water; others abstain from hard-shelled (fruit) and eggs, while others partake only of dry bread . . . and as no one can produce a written ordinance about it, it is clear that the Apostles left the matter to the judgement and disposition of each one, so that none should do good from fear or constraint' (*Eccles. Hist.* 5.22). Notwithstanding, when Socrates wrote this, there did exist a written ecclesiastical ordinance on fasting, but not universally binding. The local Council of Laodicea (360) had appointed xerophagia for all the days of the Great Forty-Day Fast (50th Canon). The term 'xerophagia' includes all vegetable foods but without oil. Such austerity did not prevail, but two other ways of fasting evolved. The first is mentioned by Theodore of Studium (ninth century), who says, when talking about the Great Lent: 'Xerophagia or beans and lentils without oil, and no wine except on Saturday and Sunday, is our fare; we also eat shellfish, all that is invertebrate, and dried fish, without any qualms'.[9] The second kind of fasting is described by John of Damascus (eighth century), who says: 'Abstinence, moreover, applies to cheese and suchlike, along with meats' (P.G. 95, 69). The prohibition of oil is not included; but it is self-evident that the permission to use oil did not apply to Wednesday and Friday.

The Apostolic Constitutions mention a fast of one week after the feast of All Saints (5, 20, 14). Since the Apostles had begun to preach after Pentecost, so the days following Pentecost were dedicated to the Apostles' memory. For this reason the fast in question was known in Syrian sources as the Fast of the Apostles, although the feast of the Holy Apostles on the 29th of June had not yet been introduced into the East. A fast was also introduced prior to Christmas, at first lasting only a few days. These two fasts, in imitation of the Easter fast, came to last forty days. They were kept in this way during the sixth century by the monks of Syria and Palestine. The first record of these two new fasts is to be found in Anastasius of Sinaï (seventh century), who lived in Syria and Egypt (P.G. 89, 668) and, following him, in Nicephorus, Patriarch of Constantinople[10] and Theodore of Studium,[11] both representatives of the monastic life of Constantinople at the end of the eighth and the beginning of the ninth century. The fast after Pentecost did not continue to be observed for a full forty days, but was curtailed. When the feast of the Holy Apostles was introduced, this fast was attached to the feast. Theodore of Studium says explicitly that, during his time, there were three fasts a year: Easter, Christmas, and the Holy Apostles;[12] he is also the first to mention another fast, 'the fast of the Mother of God', before the Dormition of the Mother of God on the 15th of August (P.G. 99, 1703). The fasts of the Holy Apostles, Christmas and the Mother of God in their full length and strictness were at first only obligatory for monks, but gradually came to be binding also on those who were not monks, both clergy and laity; this, however, came about after the twelfth century. Around the ninth century, isolated fasts are also mentioned, such as those of the Exaltation of the Cross (14th September), the eve of Epiphany, etc.

From all this it emerges that the practice of fasting within the Church underwent a development as regards the length of the fasts, the way they were kept, and the type of food used, while a gradual increase in the fasts is perceptible, primarily under the influence of the rule of the monasteries. These striking differences in fasting did not, however, harm the Church's unity. 'The disagreement on fasting is combined with agreement on faith' (Irenaeus, quoted by Eusebius). Quite apart from this development, the practice of fasting has always been an important institution for the Church, a means of spiritual elevation and of the domination of spirit over flesh, strengthening the human will and character.

The Church's patristic and liturgical tradition follows in this matter the words of our Lord, 'It is not that which passes into the mouth that defiles a man, but that which comes out of the mouth', that is, out of the heart, either good or evil; and therefore, along with abstinence from food, it emphasizes spiritual fasting, meaning abstinence from wicked acts. 'Let us keep a spiritual fast pleasing to the Lord, by abstaining from lying and false swearing . . .'; 'The Kingdom of God is not food and drink, but righteousness and asceticism combined with sanctification . . .'.[13]

The Interorthodox Preparatory Commission recognizes that most of the faithful in the society of today do not keep all the rules of fasting, on account of the difficult circumstances in which they live. Contemporary conditions demand a form of fasting that is less severe and shorter in length. Such a change is necessary in order to avoid creating problems of conscience such as result from breaking the strict ecclesiastical ordinances—problems which poison the spiritual life of the faithful.

A change in the rules of fasting currently in force does not conflict with the basic principles of fasting. The differences in the early Church over the length of the fast or the foodstuffs used, and also the development of fasting—as we have seen—did not raise any doubt about the salvation of the faithful. 'Watch out lest anyone lead you astray from this the way of the teaching. . . . If any one is capable of bearing all the yoke of the Lord, he will be perfect; and if he cannot, let him do what he can. Concerning food, let him bear it who can . . .'.[14]

The right to modify the rules on fasting and adapt them to contemporary needs belongs to the Great and Holy Council of the whole Orthodox Church.

Taking into account the relevant report of the Serbian Church, the comments of the Churches of Cyprus and Czechoslovakia, and the ensuing discussion, the Interorthodox Preparatory Commission proposes the following for further consideration:

1. All the rules on fasting currently valid are to be faithfully kept by the monks, and by as many of the clergy and laity as wish and are able to do so.

2. As regards all other Christians, who have difficulty in abiding by the strict rules on fasting that are in force, on account of special circumstances prevailing in particular places, whether because of the climate, way of life, problems of diet and difficulty in obtaining the required foods for fasting, etc.; in order to prevent the holy practice of fasting from falling into disuse among the People of God, the Commission proposes the following:

3. The Orthodox Churches may permit the eating of certain ordinary foods in order to help the faithful, but this permission should be regarded as a partial lightening of the burden according to the circumstances, as an 'indulgence' or a milder form of fasting.

4. It is proposed that the Wednesday and Friday fasts be observed throughout the year, but that oil and fish be permitted except on those Wednesdays and Fridays that fall in the periods of fasting. This permission to use oil and fish does not apply to those Wednesdays and Fridays which coincide with the Exaltation of the Holy Cross, the Beheading of St John the Baptist, and the eve of Epiphany.

5. The rules for the relaxation of the fast are valid for Wednesdays and Fridays during the weeks when fasting is relaxed. All foods may be permitted also on all Wednesdays and Fridays during the period from the Sunday of St Thomas to Ascension Day.

6. The duration of the great (40-day) Lenten fast should remain as it is, according to the regulations in the *Paschalion* (Easter table) and the *Typikon* (book of liturgical statutes). The regulations in force regarding the quantity and the type of food for the first week and the week of the Passion, are to be preserved. On other days, from the second week of the fast to Palm Sunday inclusive, fish and oil should be allowed, except for Wednesday and Friday (see clause 4).

7. As regards the Advent fast, the Interorthodox Preparatory Commission makes two suggestions: (a) either to shorten it by half (20 days), starting from the day after the feast of St Barbara, and to allow throughout the consumption of fish and oil, except for the last five days; or (b) to let it remain at 40 days, allowing fish and oil on all days except for the first three and the last three, when severe fasting is to be observed.

8. The fast of the Apostles should be limited to eight days before the feast, if a period of more than eight days intervenes between the Sunday of All Saints and the feast of the Apostles. Fish and oil should be allowed during that feast.

9. The fast prior to the 15th of August should be kept at the same length, but fish and oil should be allowed on all days except Wednesday and Friday.

10. Should the feasts of the Holy Apostles Peter and Paul or the Dormition of the Mother of God fall on a Wednesday or a Friday, the fast should be relaxed, seeing that it has been preceded by a fast preparing for the feast.

If the Panorthodox Preparatory Commission adopts these proposals, the faithful shall be duly informed of the modifications.

NOTES

1. *Teaching of the Twelve Apostles*, 8.1.

2. *Teaching of the Twelve Apostles*, cf. Tertullian, *De jejunio*, 2, Hippolytus, *Eccles. Ordinances*, ch. 47 and 55, Origen, *10th Homily on Leviticus*, P.G. 12, 528.

3. *Epistle of Irenaeus to Victor of Rome*, in Eusebius, *Eccles. History*, 5, 24, 12.

4. Dionysius of Alexandria, *Letter to Bishop Basileides*, P.G. 10, 1278.

5. Augustine, Letter 55, 28; Jerome, *Commentary on Isaiah*, ch. 58.

6. *Eccles. Hist.*, 7, 19, cf. Socrates, *Eccles. Hist.*, 5, 22, 32, P.G. 76, 631.

7. Sozomen, *Eccles. Hist.*, 7, 19, 7, cf. Socrates, *Eccles. Hist.*, 5, 22, 33.

8. John of Damascus, P.G. 95, 69; Theodore of Studium, P.G. 99, 1700.

9. *Chronicle of the Teaching of the Monastery of Studium*, P.G. 99, 1700.

10. No. 815, Rallis-Potlis, *Constitution*, 5, 428ff.

11. No. 826, P.G. 99, 1713 and 1716.

12. *Chronicle of the Teaching of the Monastery of Studium*, P.G. 99, 1693 and 1696.

13. Doxastikon of the Ainoi, 5th Sunday in Lent.

14. *Teaching of the Twelve Apostles*, VI, 1–3.

# 4

# *Impediments to marriage*

The Interorthodox Preparatory Commission of the Great and Holy Council of the Orthodox Church, after a complete study of the question of 'Impediments to Marriage', taking into account the present-day practice in the local Churches, has arrived at the following conclusions:

The Commission has based itself mainly on the special introductory reports of the Holy Churches of Russia and Greece, on the observations put forward by the holy Churches of Serbia, Romania, Bulgaria, Cyprus, Poland, and Czechoslovakia, and on the views expressed in assembly by the Orthodox representatives.

From among the impediments to marriage set out in the above recommendations and observations, the Interorthodox Preparatory Commission has selected those mentioned below, to which it gave particular attention, as being those which chiefly preoccupy the Orthodox Church today; it proposes that further study and recommendations on these points be made by the First Preconciliar Conference.

As regards impediments to marriage in general, the Church should take into account the rules of the civil legislation in each place, to the extent, naturally, to which this legislation is compatible with ecclesiastical practice.

## I  MARRIAGE BETWEEN ORTHODOX

(*a*) In the case of blood ties, there may be a relaxation of the rules as far as the 5th degree inclusive (Canon 54, Quinisext), if special circumstances render this desirable.

(*b*) In the case of collateral ties, marriage may be permitted by economy as far as the 5th degree inclusive (Canon 54, Quinisext), while marriage within the 4th degree is strictly forbidden, in accordance with the commonly accepted ancient tradition.

(*c*) In the case of relationship through adoption, marriage should be forbidden as far as and including the 2nd degree, that is, marriage by the adopter or his offspring with the adoptee.

(*d*) In the case of baptismal ties, marriage should be forbidden as far as and including the 2nd degree (Canon 53, Quinisext), that is, marriage between godfather and goddaughter or her mother and vice versa, or between godmother and godson or his father.

(*e*) Concerning relationship between in-laws, marriage at the first degree should be excluded, though it has not always been considered an absolute impediment to marriage. Nonetheless, complete indifference on the part of the Church to marriage between in-laws could have harmful results, because it would create the impression that traditions were needlessly being violated.

(*f*) Where priesthood is concerned, according to existing canons marriage is forbidden to all persons in holy orders, whatever their rank (Canon 3, Quinisext).

Nothwithstanding this, the Commission, bearing in mind the situation in some of the local Churches and the pastoral needs subsisting in different places, considers that it would advantageous for the Church to consider sympathetically the possibility of marriage after ordination for the first degree of priesthood, that is, for deacons, examining the matter in the spirit of the canons and the ancient practice of the Church, lest the ranks of the clergy be diminished in number.

(*g*) In the case of monastic orders, these constitute an absolute impediment to marriage (Canon 44, Quinisext). Monks who leave the monastic brotherhood and cast off the habit, either by their own choice or involuntarily and under constraint, may proceed to marry once they have been reinstated in the ranks of the laity by an ecclesiastical decision.

(*h*) Where an existing marriage is concerned, it constitutes an absolute impediment to entering upon another marriage, until the existing marriage shall have been irrevocably dissolved or declared null and void. The Orthodox Church forbids a fourth marriage absolutely and categorically.

(*i*) Finally, concerning the lower and upper limit of age, it is advisable to keep to the local laws of the State.

## II  MIXED MARRIAGES

(1) BETWEEN ORTHODOX AND NON-ORTHODOX

On the question of mixed marriages, the following views have been put forward:

(*a*) The Church of Russia accepts that 'marriage of Orthodox Christians with non-Orthodox Christians may be blessed in church with the ceremony of crowning, provided that the non-Orthodox partner recognizes the significance of the blessing dispensed by the Orthodox Church'.

Following upon the Roman Catholic decision to recognize the validity of marriage between Roman Catholics and Orthodox performed by an Orthodox priest, the Church of Russia has also decided to recognize the validity of mixed marriages between Orthodox and Roman Catholics performed under exceptional circumstances, after the blessing of an Orthodox bishop, before a Roman Catholic priest.

(*b*) The Church of Greece considers it advisable to avoid and discourage mixed marriages, irrespective of Churches and Confessions, and to permit them only under exceptional circumstances.

(*c*) The Church of Poland recommends that, in true ecumenical spirit, and on the basis of local interconfessional relations, mixed marriages should be permitted among all the baptized.

The Interorthodox Preparatory Commission considers it desirable that, on the basis of the above suggestions, a decision on the vexed question of mixed marriages should be taken by the First Preconciliar Conference. Since, however—as differences in the practice of the various local Churches show—there does not exist full agreement among the Orthodox on the problem, it is desirable for the First Preconciliar Conference to leave a certain amount of latitude for solving the question on the basis of local conditions. This obviously requires a more exact appreciation—so far as this is possible—of the Christian heritage of non-Orthdox Churches and an evaluation of their present circumstances, so that an ecclesiological distinction may be made among the various Christians who are not Orthodox.

(2) BETWEEN ORTHODOX AND NON-CHRISTIANS OR NON-BELIEVERS

The following views on the subject have been put forward:

(*a*) The Church of Russia affirms that such mixed marriages are forbidden by the 72nd Canon of the Quinisext Ecumenical Council, but considers nothwithstanding that 'the conditions under which the Church of God exists today upon earth urgently demand a return to the ecclesiastical practice of the first three centuries of Christianity as regards mixed marriages between Orthodox Christians and non-Christians', at which time the Church, following St Paul (1 Cor. 7.12–14, 16), 'by an exercise of condescension allowed such mixed marriages'. Besides, 'in the most ancient canons there are no regulations forbidding them'.

(b) According to the Church of Cyprus, marriage between Christians and members of other religions is forbidden (Canon 14, 4th Ecum. Council).

(c) The Church of Greece feels that on the question of marriage with non-Christians the Preconciliar Conference should be able to accept and apply the principle of economy.

(d) The Church of Poland proposes that 'the possibility should be discussed of blessing one partner in cases where the other is a non-believer'.

(e) The Church of Czechoslovakia cannot bless a mariage between an Orthodox Christian and a non-Christian (Jew, Muslim etc.).

Taking into account the above attitudes of the various Orthodox sister Churches, and after careful study of the existing Church canons, which specify that marriage between an Orthodox believer and a non-Orthodox or non-believer can take place only after the reception of the non-Orthodox or non-believer into the Church, the Commission proposes that ways and means of applying economy in this matter be studied, and that in the meantime it should be left to the local Orthodox Churches to determine whether to apply economy under circumstances of necessity.

# 5

## Concerning the calendar and the date of Easter

The Interorthodox Preparatory Commission of the Great and Holy Council has considered the following texts dealing with the 'calendar question': a study relating the question to the decision of the First Ecumenical Council concerning Easter and seeking a way to re-establish a common practice among the Churches; the introductory reports of the Churches of Russia and Greece; observations by the Churches of Romania, Bulgaria, Cyprus and Czechoslovakia; and also the views expressed by the Orthodox representatives in plenary sessions and study groups. On the strength of this, the Commission reports as follows:

The subject under study has both a theoretical (theological) and a practical (pastoral) side.

1. St Paul says: 'But now that ye have come to know God, or rather to be known of God, how turn ye back again to the weak and beggarly rudiments, whereunto ye desire to be in bondage over again? Ye observe days, and months, and seasons, and years. I am afraid for you, lest by any means I have bestowed labour upon you in vain' (Gal. 4.9–11). It is not a question of dogma but of Church order: nor do there exist any canonical ordinances concerning the calendar, with the sole exception of the date of Easter. The ancient Church followed the calendar current in the Roman Empire.

On this subject, as is well known, there is not the unity there should be among Orthodox. The local Orthodox Churches do not all employ the same calendar for the immovable feasts, nor the correct tables for ascertaining Easter as stipulated by the First Ecumenical Council of Nicaea.

The diversity of liturgical practices and ecclesiastical customs constitutes, certainly, a phenomenon acceptable in principle within the Orthodox Church, so long as beneath this diversity of outward appearances the inner organic unity of the Orthodox Church as a catholic whole is made manifest. But the existing agreements in regard to the calendar stand on an entirely different level, since they bring about a slackening of the bonds of unity. From its very beginnings, the Church tried to overcome the differences over the date of Easter. Indeed, the decision of the First Ecumenical Council of Nicaea had as its timely goal the bringing about of Christian unity through the common celebration of Easter. However, the Orthodox Churches, following either the old or the new calendar, disregard the rule laid down by Nicaea, according to which the common celebration of Easter should take place on the Sunday following the vernal equinox, after the first spring moon.

This anomaly is yet more striking if considered in the light of the contemporary astronomical advances in calendar calculation. The Church is bound to take notice of these advances, seeing that the ancient Church did so at Nicaea. That Council, as is well known, laid upon the Bishop of Alexandria the task of informing all the Churches, through annual Paschal Letters, of the proper date for celebrating Easter. This was because the bishop of Alexandria had in his city the scientific, astronomical means of calculating more precisely the spring equinox, and so the date of Easter which depended upon it. It is therefore quite evident that the First Ecumenical Council considered the astronomical factor as of prime importance for determining the common date of Easter. It thus follows that all the Orthodox Churches following the decisions of the First Ecumenical Council, are bound to celebrate Easter on the first Sunday after the full moon following the vernal equinox, according to the most precise calculations that scientific astronomy can provide. In each case, this means employing the calendar considered by expert astronomers to be the most exact. For the moment, the experts favour the new Orthodox calendar.

2. Taking the foregoing into account, and acting in the spirit of the First Ecumenical Council, the Interorthodox Preparatory Commission puts forward the following proposals:

Easter should be celebrated at one and the same time by the whole of the Orthodox Church, that is, on the first Sunday after the first full moon following the vernal equinox.

So as to apply as closely as possible the canonical ordinances linking the date of Easter to the time of the vernal equinox, a calendar as exact as possible is needed for the purpose. The current new Orthodox calendar, in the opinion of expert astronomers, is more exact than the old one. Therefore the best way of settling the question of the calendar and Easter is for all the local Orthodox Churches to adopt the new Orthodox calendar, for determining both the immovable feasts and the date of Easter. The conciliar panorthodox resolution concerning the one calendar and the date of Easter should be binding on all the local Orthodox Churches.

None the less, the Interorthodox Preparatory Commission acknowledges certain local pastoral difficulties (this emerges from a study of the report of the Russian Church, from the declaration of the Serbian Church and from the special declaration of the Patriarchate of Jerusalem), and it therefore proposes that the time and way of applying the resolution should be left to the discretion of the local Churches.

The Interorthodox Preparatory Commission notes with satisfaction the admirable practice prevailing in certain parts of the world whereby, wherever there is a local Orthodox Church using the new Orthodox calendar for determining Easter and other feasts, and there exist within its territory communities or parishes belonging to another Church, which follows the old calendar and Easter reckoning, the latter conform to the local custom. The same holds good when the roles are reversed. The Interorthodox Preparatory Commission recommends that this custom should become general in all the Orthodox Churches, as a first step towards a common celebration of Easter.

The Interorthodox Preparatory Commission also recommends that there should be joint research with non-Orthodox Christians into matters concerning the calendar and Easter so that, in the future, simultaneous celebration of the great Christian feasts by the whole of Christendom, so greatly desired by all concerned, may be brought to pass.

# 6

## *Economy in the Orthodox Church*

After studying the subject chosen by the Fourth Panorthodox Conference in Chambésy (Geneva), 'Economy in the Orthodox Church', the Interorthodox Preparatory Commission submits herewith to the First Preconciliar Panorthodox Conference, for judgement and approval, the present final draft of recommendations, as drawn up on the basis of the initial introductory report on the subject submitted by the Church of Romania, the relevant views on the topic expressed beforehand by the Church of Poland, and the opinions voiced in assembly by the various delegates.

The final draft runs thus:

## I  INTRODUCTION

The Church of Christ is the holy and infallible body within which, and through which, the work of man's salvation is realized.

The whole institution of the Church is held together and constituted by the indwelling Holy Spirit, who heals what is weak and makes up that which is wanting. The Church, as the ark of grace and truth, expressing herself through the proper channels and dispensing the treasure of divine grace, leads the faithful to salvation.

For this work the Church uses not only 'akribeia' (strict application of canon law), but also 'oikonomia' (=economy, modified and flexible application of canon law), since 'there are two kinds of government and correction in the Church of Christ: the one is called *akribeia*, the other *oikonomia* and condescension; with these the stewards (*oikonomoi*) of the Spirit guide souls to salvation now with the one, now with the other'.[1] Likewise, according to Patriarch Dositheus of Jerusalem, 'Church affairs are viewed in two ways: by *akribeia* and by *oikonomia*. So that when they cannot be settled by *akribeia*, they are settled by *oikonomia*'.[2]

## II  MEANING OF THE TERMS
## 'AKRIBEIA' AND 'OIKONOMIA'
## IN THE ORTHODOX CHURCH

The terms *akribeia* and *oikonomia* are customarily employed in theological terminology to denote two different attitudes taken by the Church in making use of the means of salvation at her disposal.

The first of the two terms, *akribeia,* denotes the Church's strict adherence to the canonical ordinances concerning each believer.[3]

The other term, *oikonomia,* denotes the Church's loving care towards her members who transgress her canonical ordinances,[4] and also towards those Christians who are outside her body and wish to enter it.[5]

### Akribeia

The whole situation and life of man in relation to God is regulated ecclesiastically according to gospel teaching and the Church's canons. This means that in the meeting between man and God who acts, the relationship is a relationship of canonicity and *akribeia.* This requires on the one hand the correct and full acceptance of revealed truth and grace, and on the other, the correct and full conformity in freedom to the canons laid down by the Church.

### Oikonomia

Apart from the meaning which concerns us here, the term *oikonomia,* also denotes the divine purpose or *prothesis* (Eph. 1.10, 3.9–11),[6] the mode of existence of the one Godhead in Trinity through mutual indwelling (*perichoresis*),[7] its broad action in the world through the Church,[8] Divine Providence,[9] the Saviour's Incarnation,[10] the whole redeeming work of our Lord Jesus Christ[11] and all the operations through which human nature was made manifest in the Son,[12] from the time of His incarnation to His ascension into heaven.[13]

In particular, the Church Fathers and other ancient ecclesiastical writers use the term *oikonomia* primarily to designate the Incarnation of our Lord as a truth of faith, contained in certain doctrinal formulations of the Ecumenical Council and in other contemporary declarations of faith.[14] The 7th Ecumenical Council uses a particular dogmatic formula to describe how faith penetrates into the 'saving economy' of our Lord Jesus Christ.[15] Economy as an object of faith is also mentioned in other texts of the 7th Ecumenical Council,[16] along with the whole redeeming work of Christ.[17]

In the same way, since the Church continues to make available to the faithful the redeeming work of our Lord Jesus Christ in the world, the holy Fathers and the ecclesiastical writers also give the name 'economy' to the work of the Church and describe it as 'saving economy', 'ecclesiastical economy', 'economy of the Church', etc.[18]

It is therefore the Church's right and mandate, copying the economy of Christ and displaying, as a mother according to grace, an especial loving-kindness, to employ economy when dealing with the divers weaknesses and shortcomings of men in their faith and the Christian life.

Economy can be regarded either as a kind of deviation from the full and exact acceptance of the saving truth—a deviation permitted to a man because of his inability to grasp this truth completely and apply it in his life; or else as a deviation from the exact and full observance of canon law. Yet at the same time economy does not abolish exactness, since the Church through her love and her sanctifying divine grace makes up all that is lacking in the life of her members.

However, things being what they are, and it being utterly impossible to broaden the content of Revelation, economy cannot be more demanding than exactness (*akribeia*), since one turns to economy precisely in situations where exactness proves impossible to apply.

## III ECONOMY IN THE SACRAMENTS WITHIN THE CHURCH AND OUTSIDE IT

Thus *akribeia* and *oikonomia* are the two poles determining the limits within which the Church's work unfolds, in regard both to her own members and to the Christians outside her ranks. They constitute the two main ways in which the Church can advance in the use of the means of salvation.

The problems concerning exactness and economy have attained vast proportions in contemporary Church life; for never before in the Church's history have the issues of inter-Church and interconfessional relations, of the *rapprochement* and union of Christians, and of ecumenical unity, been raised so persistently and in so many different guises.

The economy employed by our Holy Orthodox Church has its roots in Holy Scripture and Tradition; it has been defined and fixed by decisions of local and Ecumenical Councils and developed by the

Fathers of the Church, and also by subsequent and contemporary Orthodox theologians, and has been carried into practice by the Autocephalous Churches.

This practice has two sides to it: dogmatic and canonical. As we have said, the origin and basis of ecclesiastical economy is the Incarnation of our Lord Jesus Christ and His entire work of redemption, which started at the Incarnation as an act of divine condescension and philanthropy.[19] Ecclesiastical economy takes its origin from the spirit of God's love and mercy towards men and is governed by the same spirit, in the words of our Saviour: 'For God so loved the world, that he gave his only-begotten Son, that whosoever believeth on him might not die, but have everlasting life' (John 3.16) and 'I desire mercy, and not sacrifice' (Matt. 9.13).

The Fathers of the Church use the term 'oikonomia' above all in the sense of God's condescending to man in the Incarnation.[20] We find this sense in St Athanasius, [21] St Basil,[22] St Cyril of Alexandria,[23] Theodotus of Ancyra,[24] Maximus the Confessor,[25] St John of Damascus,[26] and St Photius.[27] Many other Fathers call the Son's Incarnation 'the mystery (or sacrament) of the economy', or 'the great mystery of the economy'—to quote the exact doctrinal terms used by the Quinisext Ecumenical Council.[28]

The divine Apostles, bearing in mind that, through the Incarnation and sacrifice of Christ the Saviour, God wants 'all men to be saved and to come to the knowledge of truth' (1 Tim. 2.4), acted through the gift of sanctifying divine grace and through various means of salvation to save straying sinners, either by the canon of *akribeia* or by the canon of *oikonomia*.

Following the example of the Apostles 'as good stewards of the manifold grace of God' (1 Pet. 4.10), the leaders of the Holy Churches during the first centuries undertook in the same way to solve the problems relating to the saving work of the Church. It is clear from the canonical and patristic works that the main purpose pursued in the practice of economy was to prevent the door of salvation being shut to anyone (1 Tim. 2.4, Acts 14.27), and to ensure on the contrary that the gates of heaven were opened wide to every believer, thereby rendering easier the return into the bosom of the Church of all who had strayed.[29]

Many are the synodical and patristic canons which make use of the term *oikonomia*, or similar terms, to describe the Church's condescension. This condescension is displayed towards not only the living but the dead as well, with a view to reinstating them after their death.

That the Church was primarily concerned with saving souls in its legislation on economy and its practice of the same is shown not only by the canons and their application but also by the way in which a whole succession of Fathers and ecclesiastical writers understood, interpreted, and applied the principle of economy. In addition to the decisions already mentioned, reference should be made also to the canonical ordinances of St Gregory of Nyssa,[30] as well as to guidelines and interpretations given by St John Chrysostom,[31] St Cyril of Alexandria,[32] Theodotus of Ancyra,[33] St John the Faster (Jejunator),[34] Eulogius of Alenandria,[35] Maximus the Confessor,[36] Anastasius of Sinai,[37] Nicephorus the Confessor,[38] Theodore of Studium,[39] St Photius,[40] Nicholas Mysticus,[41] and finally the great commentaries on the holy Canons and notably those of Zonaras,[42] Balsamon[43] and Aristenus.[44]

Particularly eloquent is the way in which the meaning and aims of economy are phrased by Nicholas Mysticus, Patriarch of Constantinople (901–6, 912–25), who writes: 'Economy is salvatory condescension, saving the man who has sinned, stretching out a helping hand to raise the fallen. . . . Economy is an imitation of divine philanthropy'.[45]

In their interpretation of many canons, Zonaras, Balsamon and Aristenus themselves stress this saving aim of economy, 'to bring back the lost sheep' to the fold of the Church.[46]

## IV  ECONOMY IN THE RECEPTION
## OF HERETICS AND SCHISMATICS
## BY THE ORTHODOX CHURCH

It can be seen from the above that there are two distinct levels on which economy is practised. The first consists of the ordinary means applied, with logic and prudence, by the Orthodox Church for the strengthening and guidance of her faithful flock along the path of salvation; while the second consists of the provision of sanctifying grace by the Church in special circumstances both to her own faithful and to those Christians outside her body who desire to enter within her bosom.

In this second case, economy reveals the Church as the ark and steward (*oikonomos*) of divine grace, dispensing it in exceptional circumstances to those who have received the sacraments either within the Church or outside it, but without fulfilling all the conditions laid down by the Church for their salvation.

Economy, as an exceptional means of salvation, goes beyond the rigid canonical bounds of *akribeia* in the sacramental life of the Church. It may thus be said that economy constitutes an exceptional type of action, yet of the same nature as the action invoked in bestowing the sacraments; it reinforces the effect of each one of the sacraments by completing or confirming them under certain circumstances, notably when they have been imperfectly performed. In this manner, economy may be considered as completing what is lacking and, through divine grace, perfecting that which has not been performed according to *akribeia*.

In ecclesiastical legislature both old and new, as in the writings of the theologians, the term *oikonomia* is used in this special sense of the dispensation by the Church of sanctifying grace exceptionally, in certain cases. The term *oikonomia* is likewise used in various other senses, also expressed by the words *synkatabasis* (condescension), *pronomion* (privilege), *epieikeia* (mildness, i.e., prudent moderation), *eleos* (mercy), *eleêmosynê* (charitable giving), *philanthropia* (philanthropy, loving-kindness), *apolysis* (loosing), *syngnômê* (pardon, forgiveness), *lysis* (freeing), *aphesis* (remission), etc. But all of these terms have their own particular meaning, which does not cover the bestowing of sanctifying grace. They are limited to matters of a disciplinary or administrative nature and, in general, to matters pertaining to canonical relations and the moral behaviour of the faithful.

The Orthodox Church has applied *akribeia* and *oikonomia* in dealing both with her own members and with non-Orthodox (heterodox). In the case of the latter, she has always clearly distinguished between the different types of heterodox whom she has received into her bosom—some of them returning in penitence to their father's house, like the Prodigal Son (Luke 6.11–32), while she has forgiven others in the name of Christ, even those who have caused her much sorrow (2 Cor. 2.5–11); for she has not considered them to be in permanent schism and separation from her, but only temporarily, 'for Satan must not be allowed to get the better of us' (2 Cor. 2.11, NEB).

The Church being one, all who are alienated from her may be considered as standing on different rungs of one and the same ladder leading up to her when they desire to return to the Church. More precisely, we could say that the Holy Spirit acts upon other Christians in very many ways, depending on their degree of faith and hope.

It is consequently clear that Christians outside the Church, even when they do not maintain their faith intact and immaculate, none the less keep their link with Christ, through their unwavering hope in Him. These Christians rejoice 'with the joy of hope' (Rom. 12.12). They confess that, through hope, they possess Christ, the common Lord, along with all Christians, because the confession of Christ unites us all, He being our common Lord and the hope of our final salvation.

To understand more clearly the relationship between the faithful outside and within the Church, we must turn to the way in which Scripture describes the joy of those who find themselves in the house and in the courts of the Lord. Within the Lord's house, light and warmth exist in abundance and strength, so that great joy is felt by those who approach.

This light shines afar, even into the outer darkness: 'The very word of him who hears the words of God, who with staring eyes sees in a trance the vision from the Almighty: How goodly are your tents, O Jacob, your dwelling-places, Israel, like long rows of palms, like gardens by a river, like lign-aloes planted by the LORD, like cedars beside the water!' (Numbers 24.4–6, NEB). The Psalmist distinguishes between the house of the Lord and His courts, saying: 'How dear is thy dwelling-place, thou LORD of Hosts! I pine, I faint with longing for the courts of the LORD's temple' (Ps. 83.1–2, NEB: Ps. 84.1–2).

The light and the joy of the Lord's house and His courts extend a long way off, inasmuch as their radiance is not abruptly blocked, nor does the outer darkness begin suddenly and all at once. In other words, the darkness of the lack of grace seeps gradually over those who are outside the Church. Grace is not completely wanting in them, because they still maintain some form of relationship with Jesus Christ and His Church, and so the light of the divine grace of the Church in some way still enlightens them.

Thus those outside the Orthodox Church can be considered as dwelling, after their departure from the Lord's house and from His courts, more or less afar off.[47]

Taking all this into account, we are convinced that all who fervently seek the revealed truth and salvation, and who are united with the Church which preserves this truth, may be saved.

The way to the Church is opened by love proceeding from faith; for 'the man who loves his brother dwells in light' (1 John 2.10), and the light leads him to union with Christ. Consequently, to evaluate the worth of sacraments performed outside the Church, apart from the criterion of faith, the Church has taken into account the presence or absence of love on the part of the believers outside her. This explains why the same local Church has at one time recognized and at another time pronounced invalid and ineffectual for salvation, the sacraments of the same heterodox, when considering their return into her bosom.

As the ark of truth and steward of divine grace, the Church, in carefully watching over the appropriation by the faithful of the faith and grace in Christ, remains on the basis of exactness (*akribeia*). But where it is permissible, or even advisable, for her to judge by herself what is best for her and for the souls entrusted to her, she uses her own discretion in administering lovingly all the means at her disposal, with the sole objective of saving the souls of her children and of facilitating her work in the Christian world understood in the wider sense.

This being the purpose of economy in the Orthodox Church, there have been two poles round which its practice within the Church has revolved:

(*a*) The first essential element taken into account in the application of economy to Christians outside Orthodoxy is the degree of closeness shown by them to the faith, doctrine and sacramental grace of the Orthodox Church.

(*b*) The second essential element is the evaluation of their feelings towards the Orthodox Church, taking into account their past actions, favourable or at least not unfavourable to Orthodoxy, also the zeal which they have displayed—officially or on a more personal level—for their incorporation into the body of our One, Holy, Catholic and Apostolic Orthodox Church.

These criteria have always been decisive in the Orthodox Church for determining whether *akribeia* or *oikonomia* should be used with regard to those outside the Church. In ancient times this was undoubtedly the case with all heretics or schismatics, with the straying or the fallen; depending how close or how far they were dogmatically from the orthodox faith; depending, too, on the greater or lesser degrees of harm they had inflicted on the body of the Church, she would treat them differently as circumstances demanded, acting and administering her affairs in the name of Christ and ever applying the principles of *akribeia* or *oikonomia* in the best interests of herself and her faithful. In so doing she used circumspection, carefully weighing up the position of those to whom she was to apply *akribeia* or *oikonomia*: this meant either recognizing their sacraments or not, and either receiving them into her bosom or else excluding them. Such was the policy of the Orthodox Church in regulating her attitude towards the great historic heresies and schisms of the first four centuries. She never departed from exactness so far as the basic elements of her faith and doctrine were concerned, but at the same time she realized the need to guard herself from the harm and hindrance which she might suffer in her work of salvation through the continuance of the heresy or schism.

This carefully balanced determination of the Church's attitude towards those who had torn themselves away from her was dictated by purely ecclesiological reasons. It was also based on the principle that, as St Basil says, nothing prescribed and institutionalized has such an objective value, that the strict letter of exactness must be observed every time, and never the loving attitude of economy. 'My opinion therefore', says the holy Father, 'is that, since nothing has been distinctly declared about them, it is our duty to reject their baptism; and if someone has received baptism from them on his coming to the Church, we should baptize him. But if this should be an obstacle to economy in general, again we must make use of custom, and follow the Fathers, who have ordered what course we should pursue. For I am under some apprehension'—Basil the Great goes on to say—'lest, in wanting to dampen their ardour over baptism, we impede them from being saved on account of the severity of our decision; besides, if they accept our baptism, we should not be displeased. For we are not bound to return them the same favour, but only to obey the strict letter (*akribeia*) of the canons. On every ground let it be enjoined that those who come to us from their baptism be anointed in the presence of the faithful, and so approach the Sacraments'.[48] This means that the early Church distinguished one basic mark (among others) which she demanded from those outside her: that they should have been baptized in the name of the Holy Trinity.

That the ancient undivided Church also sought with all her strength to preserve the peace and unity of the Church in all her relations with those more or less distant from her, and to this purpose made lavish use of economy, is evident from the 68th Canon of the local Council of Carthage and the confirming decision of the Quinisext Ecumenical Council. Here the heretics in question are the African Donatists, and their reception into the Orthodox Church was made as easy as possible: 'Since Africa is in great need, for the peace and prosperity of the Church, those Donatist clergy who, after correcting their opinion, desire to return to catholic unity—according to the will and judgement of the Catholic bishop who governs the Church in each place, provided that such action is seen to contribute to Christian peace—shall be received with their honours, as it is clear was done in ancient times in regard to the same division. Examples from many and, indeed, from virtually all the churches in Africa, in which this error has sprung up, show this to have been the practice. Not that the synod which was convened overseas to deal with this matter should be done away, but that it may remain in force for those who wish to come over to the catholic Church, so as to avoid creating any cleavage on these issues'.[49]

Such cases go to show that the Church recognized the right, as historical examples indicate, of acting with discretionary powers and employing economy in the wide-ranging problem of relations with non-Orthodox and their return to Orthodoxy.

In subsequent times our Orthodox Church has made use of the same freedom, and still continues to do so. Throughout the centuries following the period of the first historic heresies and schisms, the Church found herself divided time and again into fragments and local Christian units of a distinctly historical, regional, and ethnical character. Thus, in the period following the Fourth Ecumenical Council of Chalcedon, came into being the venerable Churches of the East, which confess the same Lord, live by the same gospel, and partake of the apostolic succession, but at various times have differed in their closeness to the Orthodox Church. While, fundamentally, never growing cold in her love for them nor diminishing in her respect for their venerable traditions, our Holy Orthodox Church has, at different times and places, varied in her attitude to them in actual practice. At times she has leant towards the demands of akribeia, calling in question not only the correctness of their doctrinal teaching but also the validity of their sacraments and even of their baptism: and on the rare occasions when this was doubted it was repeated. At other times our Holy Orthodox Church, opening wide her arms and the treasures of her love towards these Churches, and applying the orthodox principle of oikonomia, proceeded to recognize some or all of their sacraments and—always within the limits of *oikonomia*—accepted them through ecclesiastical acts and religious ceremonies of varying degree and solemnity.

These remarks hold good also for the Roman Catholic Church. In her historical relationship with the Roman Catholic Church our Holy Orthodox Church has seen the gap between them widen over the centuries, through the combination of all the well-known internal and external factors. Towards Roman Catholics, likewise, she has adopted an attitude which has varied at different times and places, even though she has always perceived their closeness in the fundamentals of faith and the economy of grace as conferred both in the sacraments and in the apostolic succession. Thus she has varied between the strict observance of *akribeia* and the circumspect use of *oikonomia*. As a result, down the centuries all the different modes of reception into Orthodoxy were tried in their case: they were received by repetition of the sacrament of baptism, by anointing with the Holy Chrism, by a fresh confession of faith, together with the sacrament of repentance, by a special form of prayer, or by the postulant's simply submitting a written request or confession of faith. In this connection it must be stressed that this wide-ranging and varied application of *oikonomia* by the Orthodox Church was due to a change in the current appreciation within the Orthodox Church of the feelings, deeds, and actions of the other party; while the non-application of *oikonomia* and a return to the stricter demands of *akribeia* were a vital necessity to the Orthodox Church when threatened at various times and in various places.

For the Churches and Confessions stemming from the Reformation—the Lutherans, Calvinists and all the others, and in particular the Anglicans—and also for the Old Catholics, roughly the same criteria and the same degree of economy prevailed. Our Holy Orthodox Church has defined and regulated in each region, as time and place demanded, her relations and contacts with them, in the spirit of economy as far as it could prevail on each occasion.

All this goes to show not only that our Holy Orthodox Church has possessed wide freedom for applying economy towards her brothers in Christ outside her embrace, but also that the same use of economy in Orthodoxy, applied in due measure and lovingly extended to all as and when it is befitting, will likewise regulate the future relations of the Orthodox Church with the other Churches and Confessions. This will continue up to the time when the various local Churches and Confessions come together and unite in the One,

Holy, Catholic, and Apostolic Church: but then in their relations there will no longer be in force any form of *oikonomia,* in the sense of a temporary measure for dealing with an anomalous situation. There will only be the *akribeia* of the one faith, expressed as a single and indivisible whole in the exactness of faith and life; and this will hold in unity the one Body of Christ.

It therefore follows that our Holy Orthodox Church, conscious of the significance and importance of present-day Christianity, not only recognizes—though being herself the One, Holy, Catholic, and Apostolic Church—the ontological existence of all these Christian Churches and Confessions, but also positively believes that all her relationships with them are founded on the quickest and most objective clarification possible of the ecclesiological question and of their doctrinal teaching as a whole. She also recognizes that *rapprochement* with them will be brought about on terms having as their centre the divine-human structure of the Church. Yet she by no means intends to forget the existence also of the multiple pastoral responsibilities belonging to the Church of Christ, comprising her duty to preach the Gospel 'unabridged', and to remove from the conscience of the faithful everywhere all manner of censure; for it is truly a scandal to them that Christians are divided, since 'Christ is not divided' (1 Cor. 1.13).

Our Holy Orthodox Church will in no way fail to apply *akribeia* to those articles of faith and sources of grace which must be upheld, yet she will not neglect to employ *oikonomia* wherever permissible in local contacts with those outside her—provided always that they believe in God adored in Trinity and the basic tenets of the Orthodox faith which follow from this, remaining always within the framework of the teaching of the ancient Church, one and indivisible.

A further goal is, on the one hand, to provide a living witness to Christ and the true faith within a secular society and a world which for the most part does not follow Christ and, on the other hand, to lead all to the one Lord, the one faith, the one baptism, the one breaking of bread, the one God and Father of all (Eph. 4. 5–6).

Acting in this way, our Orthodox Church aims at the following positive results:

(*a*) First and foremost, to preserve her own faith and doctrine unadulterated and uninfluenced by such condescension, 'in economy', to those outside her. 'For there is no room for condescension in matters of Orthodox faith; economy can only rightly be displayed where dogma is not jeopardized' (Eulogius of Alexandria).[50]

(*b*) To assess accurately the positive aspects in the faith and doctrine professed by those outside her, in their ecclesiological structure, sacramental grace, and eschatological hope, faithful to God's word and the Gospel of salvation.

(*c*) To eliminate all feelings of antagonism, violence, and self-interest, all opportunism and interference in the private affairs of each Church, all mass or individual proselytism by the well-known methods of the past, which have proved themselves undesirable, harmful, attacking the authority of the Churches, and impeding the work of union.

(*d*) To assess in all fairness the situations created in centuries past, but also in more recent times, within Orthodoxy and outside it, involving the reception by economy of the sacraments of other believers on the basis of the Church's canonical practice.

(*e*) Within the bounds of economy—identified with the extreme loving-kindness of the Godhead—to find ways and means of applying this economy to the contemporary situation of good relations between the Christian Churches, with a view to furthering all aspects of common life in Christ: ecclesiastical practice, worship, common prayer, theological collaboration and consultation, etc., until the efforts of all the Churches towards union have been crowned with success.

(*f*) To act together on particular occasions, under the presuppositions accepted by the Orthodox Church and specified above, in a spirit of mutual respect, striving, and cooperating in common for the edification of all in Christ.

This conception of Economy—applied in the Orthodox Church to her own children and to those outside her, and accompanied by exactness (*akribeia*), which alone is valid in matters of faith and doctrine—is a special feature of Orthodoxy. It is derived from Holy Scripture and Sacred Tradition, and it takes as it were tangible form and finds its justification in the words of the Fathers and the canons of the Church. From the viewpoint of divine right it extends back as far as the Apostles and Our Lord, while from the viewpoint of the Christian's approach to his neighbour it constitutes the only means whereby the Church makes allowance for human weakness, and the human element finds the possibility of drawing near to the divine.

Thus, if *akribeia* is the chief ecclesiological mark of the One, Holy, Catholic, and Apostolic Church where the revealed truth and ever-abounding grace of the Triune God are concerned, *oikonomia* in the Church is her peculiar prerogative derived from tradition, whereby her prudence, wisdom, pastoral openness and power to make allowances wherever applicable reach their full expression, so that the work of man's salvation on earth may come to fulfilment and all things may be reconciled in Christ at the last day.

## NOTES

1. *The Rudder of the one, holy, catholic and apostolic Church of the ortho-dox* . . . by Agapios and Nikodemos, 2nd ed., Athens 1841, p. 34.

2. *Letter to Michael of Belgrade,* May 1706, publ. by K. Delikanis, *Patriarchal Documents,* Constantinople 1905, vol. III, p. 684.

3. See Canons XLVI, XLVII, LVXIII of the Holy Apostles; III and IV of Gregory of Nyssa; I, III, X, XLVII of St Basil the Great; *Letter of the 3rd Ecumenical Council,* cf. Rallis-Potlis, *Constitution of the sacred and holy Canons,* vols. II, III, IV.

4. See Canons II and V of Ancyra; XI and XII of the 1st Ecumenical Council; I and V of Gregory of Nyssa; III, V, VII, X, XVII, XVIII etc. of St Basil; II of Cyril of Alexandria; XVI of the 4th Ecumenical Council; III, XXIX, XXX, CII of the 6th Ecumenical Council, etc. in Rallis-Potlis, op. cit., vols. III, II, IV and II.

5. See Canons VIII and XIX of the 1st Ecum. Council, VII of the 2nd Ecum. Council; I and XLVII of St Basil; 6th Ecum. Council, cf. Rallis-Potlis, vols. II, IV.

6. Cf. Clement of Alexandria, *Stromateis* I, 17, Migne P.G. 8, 800–801 and Cyril of Alexandria, *Letters,* XLI, P.G. 77, 217.

7. Tertullian, *Adv. Prax.* 2; St Basil, Letters, Second Series, CLXXXIX 7, P.G. 32, 693.

8. Clement of Alex., *Strom.* I, 17, P.G. 8, 800–801.

9. Clement of Alex., *Strom.* 7, 12, P.G. 9, 501; Andrew of Caesarea in Cappadocia, *Commentary on the Apocalypse,* P.G. 106, 385.

10. St Athanasius the Great, *Letters to Serapion,* IV, 14, P.G. 26, 656, St Basil, *On the Holy Spirit,* 16, 39, P.G. 32, 140; Cyril of Alex., varia, in P.G. 76, 16, 17, 40, 148, 209, 212, 300, 301, 304, 320, 341, 417, 424, 1177, 1185, 1340, 1388 and P.G. 77, 16, 132 etc; Maximus the Confessor, *On Theology and the Economy of the Son's Incarnation,* 18, 23, P.G. 90, 1133, 1136; John of Damascus, *An Exact Exposition of the Orthodox Faith,* 3, 1, *On the Divine Economy,* 1, 2, 5, 12, 17, 28, P.G. 94, 981, 988, 1000, 1069, 1100; Photius, *Amphilochia,* quest. 1, 61, 14, P.G. 101, 48, 64–65; Id. *Bibliotheca,* 227, 230 etc., P.G. 103, 953, 1025, 1028.

11. Clement of Alex., *Strom.* 2, 5, P.G. 8, 952; Gregory of Nazianzus, Sermon 38, 14, P.G. 36, 329.

12. St Athanasius, *Commentary* on the 67th Psalm, P.G. 27, 300; Cyril of Alex., *Against Nestorius,* bk. 1, 4, P.G. 76, 40, *Exegesis of the XII Anathemas,* 2,

3, 4, P.G. 76, 300, 301, 304; *Defence of the XII Anathemas against Theodoret*, P.G. 77, 417, 424, 425, Anastasius of Sinai, *On the Economy*, 1, P.G. 89, 85.

13. Cyril of Alex., *On the Trinity*, 26, P.G. 77, 1169; John of Damascus, *Expos. Orth. Faith*, 3, 2, 3, 5, 3, 17, P.G. 94, 988, 1032, 1069 etc.; Photius, *Amphilochia*, 14, P.G. 101 65.

14. St Basil, Letters, Second Series, CCXLIII, 1, P.G. 32, 904, CCLXV, 3, P.G. 32, 989; Photius, *Bibl.*, 227, P.G. 103, 953, 956; Canon I, 6th Ecum. Council.

15. Mansi 13, 129.

16. Mansi 12, 1010, 1038ff.

17. See Canons II and V of Ancyra with the commentaries of Zonaras and Balsamon, Rallis-Potlis vol. III, pp. 23, 32 and IV, p. 33. See also the comments of Aristenus on Canon V of Ancyra; Canons XI and XII of 1st Ecum. Council, the latter with comments of Aristenus, in Rallis-Potlis, vol. II, p. 143; Canons I, III, and X of St Basil; Canon XXIX of 6th Ecum. Council; Matthew Blastares, Constitution, section M. ch. vii, in Rallis-Potlis, vol. VI, pp. 364–366.

18. See Canons III and X of St Basil, III and IV of Gregory of Nyssa, XV of 4th Ecum. Council, III and XXIX of 6th Ecum. Council, CII of 6th Ecum. Council.

19. St Basil, *On the Holy Spirit*, ch. xvii, 39, P.G. 32, 140; Cyril of Alex., *Against Nestorius*, bk. I, i, 4ff, P.G. 76, 16, 17, 40ff.

20. Cyril of Alex., *On the Trinity*, xiv, P.G. 77, 1149; Theodotus of Ancyra, *On the Nicene Creed*, 2, 5, 7, P.G. 77, 1317, 1320, 1324; Maximus the Confessor, *Two Hundred Chapters*, 2nd century, 18, P.G. 90, 1133; Anastasius of Sinai, *On the Economies*, I, P.G. 89, 85; John of Damascus, *Exposition*, bk. III, i, P.G. 94, 984.

21. *Letters to Serapion*, IV, 14, P.G. 26, 656, xvi, 39; *Commentary* on Pss. LXVII and LXXI, P.G. 27, 300, 325.

22. *On the Holy Spirit*, viii, 18, P.G. 32, 100, 140.

23. *Against Nestorius*, bk. I, 3, 5, P.G. 76, 16, 17, 40, 148, 209, 212, and *Exegesis of the XII Anathemas and Defence of the XII Anathemas*, P.G. 36, 300, 301, 304, 320ff.

24. *On the Nicene Creed*, 2, 5, 7, 8, 18, 20, 21, 22ff, P.G. 77, 1317, 1324, 1345ff.

25. *Two Hundred Chapters*, 2nd century, 23, 24, P.G. 90, 1136.

26. *Exposition*, bk. II, ii, v, xii, xvii, xxviii, P.G. 94, 988, 1000, 1032ff.

27. *Amphilochia*, quest. I, 14, XLIII, 13, 14, 16, P.G. 101, 63, 320, 321, 325, 932.

28. See Canon I.

29. See Canon CII of the Quinisext Ecum. Council.

30. Canons I-V and VI-VIII.

31. P.G. 49, 405, 408 and 61, 640.

32. P.G. 77, 248, 249, 300, 320, 321, 344, 345, 349, 353, 376.

33. P.G. 77, 1317, 1320, 1324ff.

34. Rallis-Potlis, vol. IV, 423–446.

35. P.G. 86, II, 2940 and P.G. 103, 953–956.

36. P.G. 90, 1133, 1136.

37. P.G. 89, 85.

38. Rallis-Potlis, vol. IV, 427ff and P.G. 100, 377-393.

39. P.G. 99, 1072-1084.

40. P.G. 101, 64 and P.G. 102, 773, 776; P.G. 103, 953-956, 1025, 1028.

41. P.G. 111, 212, 213.

42. Rallis-Potlis, vol. II, 210, 257, 367, 369, 551-552; III, 23, 32; IV, 93, 100, 211, 311-312.

43. Rallis-Potlis vol. II, 213-214, 368, 370, 553; III, 23; IV, 101, 312-314.

44. Rallis-Potlis, vol. II, 142-143; III, 33; IV, 94, 199-211.

45. P.G. 111, 212-213.

46. Rallis-Potlis, vol. II, 552-554.

47. Photius, *Bibl.*, 227, P.G. 103, 953–956.

48. Rallis-Potlis, IV, 91-92.

49. Rallis-Potlis, III, 476.

50. Eulogius of Alexandria, P.G. 103, 953.